AROUND philadelphia WITH KIDS

by Andrea Lehman

Fodor's Travel Publications
New York • Toronto • London • Sydney • Auckland

www.fodors.com

CREDITS
Writer: Andrea Lehman

Series Editor: Karen Cure
Editor: Linda Cabasin
Editorial Production: Linda K. Schmidt
Production/Manufacturing: Yexenia Markland

Design: Fabrizio La Rocca, *creative director*;
Tigist Getachew, *art director*
Illustration and Series Design: Rico Lins, Keren Ora
Admoni/Rico Lins Studio

ABOUT THE WRITER
Having edited eight other books in Fodor's *Around the City with Kids* series, Trenton resident Andrea Lehman relished the opportunity to write about her own backyard. When she's not editing or writing, she likes nothing better than traipsing around the Philadelphia metro area with her two daughters, discovering hidden treasures and rediscovering old favorites.

Fodor's Around Philadelphia with Kids

Copyright © 2001 by Fodors LLC

ISBN 0–679–00724–5
ISSN 1533-5305
First Edition

Important Tip
Although all prices, opening times, and other details in this book are based on information supplied to us at press time, changes occur all the time in the travel world, and Fodor's cannot accept responsibility for facts that become outdated or for inadvertent errors or omissions. So always confirm information when it matters, especially if you're making a detour to visit a specific place.

Special Sales
Fodor's Travel Publications are available at special discounts for bulk purchases for sales promotions or premiums. Special editions, including personalized covers, excerpts of existing guides, and corporate imprints, can be created in large quantities for special needs. For more information, contact your local bookseller or Special Markets, Fodor's Travel Publications, 280 Park Avenue, New York, NY 10017. Inquiries from Canada should be directed to your local Canadian bookseller or sent to Random House of Canada, Ltd., Marketing Dept., 2775 Matheson Boulevard East, Mississauga, Ontario L4W 4P7. Inquiries from the United Kingdom should be sent to Fodor's Travel Publications, 20 Vauxhall Bridge Road, London, England SW1V 2SA.

PRINTED IN THE UNITED STATES OF AMERICA
10 9 8 7 6 5 4 3 2 1

COUNTDOWN TO GOOD TIMES

GET READY, GET SET!

Everyone knows that organizing a family's schedule is a full-time job. Pickups, drop-offs, school, parties, after-school activities—everyone off in their own direction. Of course, it's an organizer's dream, but a scheduling nightmare. Spending time together shouldn't be another thing to have to figure out.

We know what it's like to try to find good places to take your children or grandchildren. Sometimes it's tough to change plans when you suddenly hear about a kid-friendly event; besides, a lot of those events end up being crowded or, worse, sold out. It's also hard to remember places you read about in a newspaper or magazine, and sometimes just as hard to tell from the description what age group they're geared to. There's nothing like bringing a "grown-up" 12-year-old to an activity that's intended for his 6-year-old sister. Of course, if you're visiting Philadelphia, it's even harder to figure out the best things to do with your kids before you even get there. That's where we come in.

What you'll find in this book are 68 ways to have a terrific couple of hours or an entire day with your children or your grandchildren. We've scoured the city, digging out activities your kids will love—from the historic buildings of Independence National Historical Park to the newfangled technology at the Franklin Institute. The best part is that it's stress-free, uncomplicated, and easy for you. Open the book to any page and find a helpful description of a kid-friendly attraction, with age ratings to make sure it's right for your family, smart tips on visiting so that you can get the most out of your time there, and family-friendly eats nearby. The address, telephone number, open hours, and admission prices are all there for your convenience. We've done the work, so you don't have to.

Naturally you'll still want to keep an eye out for seasonal events that fit your family's interests, from the annual Philadelphia Flower Show to Devon's horse shows. New Year's Day brings the over-the-top feathered and sequined Mummers Parade, while in June, an entirely different group—world-class cyclists—takes over Philly's streets for the First Union U.S. Pro Cycling Championship. Even before the family entertainment center at Penn's Landing is finished, you can check out the summer weekend children's activities there. And older, artistically minded kids might enjoy combing Old City galleries on First Friday (the first Friday of each month from 5 to 9), when galleries host openings and receptions. Pick-your-own farms bring produce to your fingertips at certain times of year, and seasonal festivals pop up in towns and shopping meccas, such as Lahaska's Peddler's Village (check out the scarecrows in fall). If you can get a group together—sometimes as few as five people—you can often take advantage of group tours offered by places as varied as KYW-TV and the main post office at 30th and Market.

WAYS TO SAVE MONEY

We list only regular adult, student (with I.D.), and kids' prices; children under the ages specified are free. It always pays to ask at the ticket booth whether any discounts are offered for a particular status or affiliation (but don't forget to bring your I.D.). Discounts are often available for senior citizens, AAA members, military personnel, and veterans, among others. Many attractions offer family memberships, generally good for one year of unlimited use for your family. These memberships sometimes allow you to bring a guest. Prices vary, but the memberships often pay for themselves if you visit the attraction several times a year. Sometimes there are other perks: newsletters or magazines, members-only previews, and discounts at a gift shop, for parking, or for birthday parties or special events. If you like a place when you visit, you can sometimes apply the value of your one-day admission to a membership if you do it before you leave.

Look for coupons—which can often save you $2–$3 per person—everywhere from the local newspaper to a supermarket display to your pediatrician's office. In addition, sometimes groups of attractions get together and offer combination tickets, which are cheaper than paying for each one individually. One such bargain is CityPass, which covers admission to six local attractions—the Academy of Natural Sciences, Franklin Institute, Independence Seaport Museum, New Jersey State Aquarium & Camden Children's Garden, Philadelphia Museum of Art, and Philadelphia Zoo—for about half the cost of separate entry. You can buy CityPass at any of these places.

Also keep an eye out for attractions—mostly museums and cultural destinations— that offer free or discounted admission one day a month, particular days of the week, or at a certain time. We've noted some in this book.

WHEN TO GO

With the exception of seasonal attractions, kid-oriented destinations are generally busiest when children are out of school—especially weekends, holidays, and summer—but not necessarily. Attractions that draw school trips can be swamped with clusters of sometimes-inconsiderate children tall enough to block the view of your preschooler. But school groups tend to leave by early afternoon, so weekdays after 2 during the school year can be an excellent time to visit museums, zoos, and aquariums. For outdoor attractions, it's good to visit after a rain, since crowds will likely have cleared out.

The hours we list are the basic hours, not necessarily those applicable on holidays. Some attractions are closed when schools are closed, but others add extra hours on these days. It's always best to check if you want to see an attraction on a holiday.

SAFETY

Obviously the amount of vigilance necessary will depend on the attraction and the ages of your kids. In crowded attractions, keep an eye on your children at all times, as their ages warrant. When you arrive, point out what the staff or security people are wearing, and find a very visible landmark to use as a meeting place, should you get separated. If you do split into groups, pick a time to meet. This will decrease waiting time, help you and your kids get the most out of your time there, and manage everyone's expectations.

FINAL THOUGHTS

Actually, this time it's yours, not ours. We'd love to hear what you or your kids thought about the attractions you visited. Or if you happened upon a place that you think warrants inclusion, by all means, send it along, so the next family can enjoy Philadelphia even more. You can e-mail us at editors@fodors.com (specify the name of the book on the subject line), or write to us at *Fodor's Around Philadelphia with Kids,* 280 Park Avenue, New York, NY 10017. We'll put your ideas to good use. In the meantime, have fun!

THE EDITORS

ACADEMY OF NATURAL SCIENCES

Something old, something new. This natural history museum provides both, in its collections—from dinosaur bones to living animals—and exhibits. Like many Philly institutions, the museum (founded 1812) is the oldest of its kind, in this case the oldest science research institution in the Western Hemisphere. In some areas, its age shows: Dioramas with posed stuffed animals remind parents of the museums of their youth. However, three exhibits provide the hands-on experiences modern museum goers expect.

Start in Dinosaur Hall (at the parkway entrance) with its large gigantosaurus and T-rex skeletons. Enter the Time Machine, a room at the far end, and you'll be transported to the Mesozoic era. Watch a monitor and try to stay calm as velociraptors and triceratops pass by. Then head upstairs to the Big Dig, where kids don goggles and, with chisel and brush, excavate dinosaur fossils (casts, actually) from a simulated dig site. Some children flit from bone to bone; others stay in a spot for hours. Helpful staff make the experience fun, encouraging kids to figure out the body part and type of dinosaur they're uncovering.

EATS FOR KIDS On ground level, a large animated apatosaurus model tilts its head, moves its eyes, opens its mouth, and screeches, perhaps because it's hungry after 65 million years. Unfortunately, it's incapable of moving the few yards over to the cafeteria-style museum *café*, which serves hamburgers, hot dogs, sandwiches, and salads. Down the parkway, **T.G.I. Friday's** (1776 Ben Franklin Pkwy., tel. 215/665–8443) has a large regular menu along with kids' fare and crayons, while **Subway** (1701 Ben Franklin Pkwy., tel. 215/568–7676) turns out subs, er, hoagies (this is Philadelphia). Also see options under the Franklin Institute and Please Touch Museum.

1900 Benjamin Franklin Pkwy.

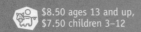 $8.50 ages 13 and up,
$7.50 children 3–12

 M–F 10–4:30, Sa–Su 10–5

215/299–1000

2 and up

In the hothouse that is Butterflies (80°F and 80% humidity), brilliantly colored tropical butterflies flutter by amid lush plantings, pausing to sip nectar from hibiscus or dine on rotting fruit (yum!). Since the butterflies are used to people, you can get close, but please don't touch them. Here, too, knowledgeable and enthusiastic staff tell (and show) all about these amazing, delicate creatures.

Outside-In, for preschool and elementary ages, is as much play area as museum. Children can make fossil rubbings, sift sand for sharks' teeth and then identify the species, or watch live animals from tarantulas to tortoises. Some (though not all) staff enjoy engaging children, sometimes letting kids handle the animals. "Look mom, I held a cockroach!" shrieked one little girl—a Madagascar hissing cockroach at that. The experience, like many here, is not something your child, or you, will soon forget.

KEEP IN MIND

In addition to the main Museum Shop, which can be patronized or avoided about as easily as any museum's store, the academy has two smaller shops, including one you must walk through upon exiting Butterflies. It's a surprising manipulation in this otherwise uncommercial institution.

HEY, KIDS! If it's live animals you're interested in, attend one of the Mini Shows held around the museum. To see animals off-duty, descend to the ground-floor Live Animal Center. Over 100 animals who can't survive in the wild—because they were injured, orphaned, or no longer wanted as pets—live here when they're not being used for education programs or birthday parties. Look through windows at their cages. Read answers to questions other kids have asked (or submit your own). You can even learn more about the care of these creatures at a daily "Meet the Keeper" talk.

AMERICAN HELICOPTER MUSEUM

The Chinese flying top, a simple propeller blade on a stick that children set flying by spinning between their hands, dates from 1100 and costs $1.59 in the museum's gift shop. Outside on the tarmac, the V-22 Osprey, a cavernous aircraft that can take off like a helicopter and fly like a jet, was built for the marines in the 1990s at a cost of about $36 million. In between these extremes, different rotary-wing aircraft—36 in all—are on display at this hangar-like museum, the only U.S. museum dedicated solely to helicopters.

The museum's full name includes "and Education Center," and teaching about helicopter history is part of its mission. You can learn about the human-powered aerial screw Leonardo da Vinci designed (but never built) in the 15th century, preceding Sikorsky's practical motorized single-rotor helicopter by over 450 years. Docents are generally available to answer questions and, if it's not too busy, take you around.

GETTING THERE The museum is about 25 miles west of Philadelphia. Take U.S. 202 to the Boot Road exit (east). Make a right on Wilson Boulevard, the next left onto Airport Road, and right again on American Boulevard. The museum is the second building on your left.

HEY, KIDS! What's the difference between an autogiro, a helicopter, and a chopper? An autogiro is air powered. Press the button on the small wind tunnel near the museum entrance. When the wind blows, the autogiro model's blades turn, actually lifting it off the ground. A helicopter's rotor, on the other hand, is turned by a motor rather than the movement of the air itself. As for a chopper, that was a trick question; chopper is just another name for helicopter.

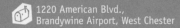 1220 American Blvd.,
Brandywine Airport, West Chester

 610/436–9600

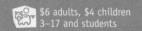 $6 adults, $4 children
3–17 and students

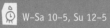 W–Sa 10–5, Su 12–5

 2 and up

You'll see many sizes and configurations of flying machine here: the Pitcairn Autogiro PCA-1A (1929), the oldest practical U.S.-built rotary craft in existence; the Sikorsky S-51 (1946), the first commercial chopper; the funky Princeton Air Cycle, a college project; the Bell H-13, best known from the TV series *M*A*S*H;* and the tandem-rotor AirGeep, an actual flying Jeep used for reconnaissance. But to the museum's core audience—preschoolers to preteens—the big attractions are the five helicopters that you can climb in: "Cheerful Chopper," "Stubby," a pair of two-seaters whose rotors tilt, and a big Navy rescue helicopter. The rescue chopper has enough room for a pilot, copilot, and several co-copilots, who can double as shipwreck victims plucked from the sea. Any kid who has ever eyed a plane cockpit with awe will love flipping switches in this one.

Little ones ready to become junior aerospace engineers or just ready to relax and draw can head to a play area, where they can design and color their own copter. Give the drawing to a docent for posting; it might just put your child's head in the clouds.

EATS FOR KIDS A small room has vending machines for snacks and soda, and you may bring lunch and eat there. Other local options include **Pizzabilities** (1149 West Chester Pike, tel. 610/692–8999), for not just pizzas (sandwiches, too); **Ron's Schoolhouse Grille** (1257 West Chester Pike, tel. 610/719–9900), for not just grills (pizza and hoagies, too); and the **Ice Cream Company** (11 N. Five Points Rd., tel. 610/696–8883) for, yup, not just ice cream (good sandwiches, soups, and salads, also).

ARDEN CHILDREN'S THEATRE

Until recently, there was a surprising lack of resident professional children's theater in Philadelphia. Enter the Arden Theatre, which began staging plays specifically for kids and families in 1998 and has expanded the series since then.

What distinguishes the Arden from the more modest, fairy-tale-on-a-shoestring kind of children's theater are its production quality, inventiveness, and, sometimes, subject matter. The company aims for the same high standards—the same caliber of actors and production value (read: the same budget)—as it does for its main-stage productions. Its goal is not just to entertain but also to educate and inspire and as a result to influence the next generation of (hopefully) sophisticated theatergoers. Considering that, tickets to ACT productions are relatively affordable.

A combination of evening and matinee performances takes place in either the 400-seat F. Otto Haas Stage or the more intimate, upstairs 175-seat Arcadia Stage. After each

KEEP IN MIND Though seating in the smaller Arcadia Stage is by general admission, you don't need to worry about arriving extra early to snag a good seat. All vantage points are close enough to the stage for kids to see well, though the occasional adult head in front of your small one might necessitate a bit of seat shifting. Seating is assigned in the larger F. Otto Haas Stage, which can be modified for thrust, in the round, or proscenium configurations. Seats are more raked here, affording good sight lines throughout. Both theaters have comfortable chairs.

40 N. 2nd St.

 215/922-8900,
215/922-1122 box office

 $22–$34 adults,
$15–$18 youths 13–
17, $12–$14 children
12 and under

 T–Su, performance times vary

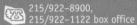 Varies by production

performance, the cast comes out for a 10- to 15-minute Q & A session, during which kids can ask anything they want—about the play's plot or theme, the craft of acting, or the behind-the-scenes secrets of how certain effects are created.

Productions are varied, as are their running times and the ages they're "best enjoyed by." When familiar stories are told, they are told in new and creative ways. One year's calendar ranged from the magical—an original adaptation of *The Snow Queen* (ages 5 and up)—to the all-too-real *And Then They Came for Me* (ages 9 and up), a gripping, unnerving, and yet moving story about two of Anne Frank's friends who survived the Holocaust. At press time, plans were under way for three children's productions per year, each running seven to eight weeks. In addition, some of the Arden's main-stage productions are appropriate for children 12 and up, resulting in about eight months of potentially kid-accessible theater per year. Exit smiling.

HEY, KIDS! Too shy to talk in public? After the Q&A session, the actors (many of whom are pretty young themselves) go into the lobby, where you can ask them questions in person, tell them how you liked the play, or just give your favorite character a hug.

EATS FOR KIDS **Margherita Pizzeria** (60 S. 2nd St., tel. 215/922–7053), formerly Larry's, has great pies: traditional pizzas with toppings from anchovies to yellow peppers plus gourmet pizzas. **Lamberti's Cucina** (212 Walnut St., 2nd fl., tel. 215/238–0499) serves kids spaghetti, ravioli, and even chicken fingers for the rare non-pasta-lover. For more local options, see other Old City listings, such as the Betsy Ross House, Fireman's Hall, Franklin Court, Independence National Historical Park, Lights of Liberty, the National Liberty Museum, Mum Puppettheatre, and the U.S. Mint.

ATSION RECREATION AREA

Though there are plenty of public swimming pools around Philadelphia, there aren't a whole lot of beaches this side of the Jersey shore. Even at the ocean, you won't find many places to swim in red water. For that you'll have to come to the recreation area at Atsion Lake, part of New Jersey's Wharton State Forest.

Yes, the water is indeed somewhere between the color of birch beer and iced tea, but it's not some horrible mutant pollution that tints it, but rather tannic acid, a product of fallen leaves and cedar roots that leaches into the water. Many of the Pine Barrens' waterways are this tawny color. It's perfectly safe and more than a little cool. Trees surround the lake and create a serene backdrop, but the serenity is quickly broken by the sounds of traffic from nearby 206 and of children on the beach. The recreation area can and does get pretty crowded on warm summer days. In fact, it often fills up and closes to new visitors on Sundays and holidays. Plan accordingly.

GETTING THERE Travel east on Route 70 to the Red Lion circle. From there proceed south on U.S. 206. The Atsion office is on the left at mile marker 7.5, and the entrance to the recreation area is a few hundred yards farther ahead on the right.

KEEP IN MIND Wharton State Forest is much bigger than just the Atsion Recreation Area. It contains four canoeable rivers that are free and open 24/7 as well as Historic Batsto Village, a state historic site in the town of the same name. Formerly a bog-iron and glass-making center, Batsto is home to 40-some structures that reflect how life was here in the late 19th century. In addition to a mansion, which you can tour, facilities include a gristmill, various barns and houses, and a sawmill.

715 U.S. 206, Shamong, NJ

 $5 per vehicle M–F,
$7 per vehicle Sa–Su

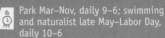 Park Mar–Nov, daily 9–6; swimming and naturalist late May–Labor Day, daily 10–6

609/268-0444

All ages

You can while away the day playing on the sandy beach and in the lake, at either of the two playgrounds, or on the playing field. A full-time naturalist leads nature walks, nature crafts, and various other activities, like scavenger hunts—check the schedule for specifics. Or drop a line for fish or bring a canoe or kayak (no motors allowed) and launch it at the boat ramp. (For a list of local canoe rental outfits, as well as maps, schedules, wildlife guides, and other information, stop at the park office, across the road. The closest outfitter is Adams Canoe Rental, 1005 Atsion Rd., Vincentown, tel. 609/268–0189.) And since the recreation area's bathhouse comes complete with showers, you don't have to return home with sand in your suit—unless you want to.

EATS FOR KIDS Aside from lots of picnic tables surrounding the parking lot, the recreation area has a snack bar that sells the usual suspects. This part of New Jersey is also diner-land, and you can take your pick of family-style diners and truck stops along U.S. 206. Two reasonable options are the **Shamong Diner** (U.S. 206, tel. 609/268–1182), a mile or so to the north, and the **Wagon Wheel** (750 U.S. 206, Hammonton, tel. 609/561–8701), to the south.

BETSY ROSS HOUSE

Of all the famous Colonial and Revolutionary names you learned about in school, there's probably only one woman. Neither a statesman nor a soldier, she was a simple seamstress, and her claim to fame was sewing the flag that became our nation's emblem. However, the main story told at Betsy Ross's house—not actually *her* house at all, but that of her landlady, the widow Lithgow—isn't about the flag or the movers and shakers of the late 18th century. It's about what a working woman's house and life would have been like.

The house is open for self-guided tours, and since it's not a big place, you won't need much time to get through it. Pause long enough to focus on the objects in the various rooms (all behind glass) and question how they're the same as, or different from, what we use today. What articles in her sewing shop have and haven't changed? Why are the stairs so narrow? Notice the curtains surrounding her bed; what do you suppose they were used for?

HEY, KIDS! Signs in the house are in the first person, as if written by Betsy herself. Sometimes they say "thee" or "thou" where we would say "you," because that was how Quakers talked in those days. Betsy Ross (original name: Elizabeth Griscom) was born a Quaker, but when she married her first husband, John Ross (an Anglican), she was "read out of meeting," which means she was kicked out of the church. She eventually married two more husbands, outliving them all, and did return to the Quaker faith. Her grave, along with that of her third husband, is in the courtyard.

239 Arch St.

 215/686-1252

 Free

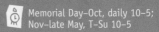 Memorial Day–Oct, daily 10–5;
Nov–late May, T–Su 10–5

 5 and up

If you come in the off-season, be prepared to combine your visit with stops at other nearby sights, as the house itself doesn't have enough to occupy you for very long. If you come in summer, however, the courtyard will be bustling with things to watch. This is the epicenter of the Town Crier Summer Theatre's family programs. You can talk to Betsy about the real story behind the flag (her grandson embroidered upon the legend many years later) and how she came up with five- rather than six-pointed stars. On the courtyard stage, you could see a Yankee Doodle puppet show, a Colonial conjurer (a magician, in modern-day English), the Libertytones singing group, or a fife and drum performance. Your kids might even learn to bow or curtsy as part of a skit on Colonial manners, practice fencing footwork after a swordplay demonstration, or get a role in a small play. You could indeed be pleasantly diverted for some time.

EATS FOR KIDS
Old City Pizza (3rd and Arch Sts., tel. 215/574–9494) is a big-menu pizza joint that goes beyond pies to include Philly steaks, deli sandwiches, hoagies, seafood, chicken, and Greek and Italian specialties. See other Old City sights for more choices.

KEEP IN MIND The Betsy Ross House is owned by the city of Philadelphia and operated by Historic Philadelphia, Inc., the same people who put on the Town Crier Summer Theatre (*see below*). Admission is free, but a suggested donation of $2 for adults and $1 for children is requested to help pay for the site's operation. Although this is one of those places where the exit takes you right through the gift shop, in this case it's hard to quibble. The vast majority of the house's expenses for infrastructure and programming are paid for with gift shop sales.

BRANDYWINE RIVER MUSEUM

In a Civil War–era gristmill on the banks of the Brandywine River, a charming three-story museum showcases the artistic heritage of the Brandywine Valley. It's a small and manageable place, one that provides a good introduction for budding art-museum goers. The museum also offers a bonus: As part of a larger nature conservancy, it has wildflower gardens and a lovely trail along the river. What better way to learn about art than to follow up a museum visit with a walk in the very countryside that inspired some of the works on display.

Of the artists represented in the permanent collection, the most famous are undoubtedly the Wyeth family, especially Andrew Wyeth. But kids seem more interested in the works of his father, N.C., and his son, Jamie. N.C. is best known for his swashbuckling illustrations for such adventure books as *Treasure Island, Kidnapped,* and *White Fang.*

EATS FOR KIDS The Museum Restaurant (tel. 610/388–8373), in a glass tower overlooking the river, offers reasonably priced lunch. **Hank's Place** (U.S. 1 and Rte. 100, tel. 610/388–7061) dishes up hearty homestyle cooking and the "What'll ya have, hon?" rural flavor of old Chadds Ford.

KEEP IN MIND Different seasons bring different reasons to visit. If you want to explore the outdoors, including the wildflower gardens, come spring–autumn. Perhaps the best time to come with kids, however, is at Christmas (late November–early January), when the whole 2nd-floor gallery is given over to model trains. Kids stand transfixed watching (and counting the cars on) trains that wind around more than 2,000 feet of O-gauge track, through tunnels, and past a refinery and dairy farm. A Victorian dollhouse is displayed, and Christmas trees are trimmed with delightful critter ornaments made from natural materials (for sale in the gift shop).

U.S. 1, Chadds Ford

610/388-2700

$5 ages 13 and up,
$2.50 children 6–12
and students

 Daily 9:30–4:30

3 and up

(You can find many of these illustrated novels along with plenty of art books in the gift shop.) If your children know any of these stories, the portraits of pirates and mountain men will come alive all the more for them. Jamie Wyeth's kid-friendly works include a life-size painting of a pig so real you could almost swear you heard her grunt. And these aren't the only artists who can appeal to children. Pick up a copy of "A Family Guide" (available in the gift shop for $1.95); this museum activity book helps kids really stop and look at selected works, learn more about the elements of art, and have fun during and after their visit.

If and when attention begins to wane, just head outside to the peaceful River Trail, which runs for about a mile. It's a sure cure for cranky kids.

HEY, KIDS! Don't hog the hog. Outside by the river are two bronze statues: Helen (a pig) and Miss Gratz (a cow). Unlike the don't-touch pictures inside, these statues aren't just hands-on; they're bottom-on. And you won't be the only one sitting on them. So many kids have sat on Helen that the bristles on her back and tips of her ears are polished shiny. Now look around her eyes and on her sides. The green color there is called patina (pronounced puh-*tee*-nuh). It's what happens to bronze with age. So be nice to the sow, and remember to take turns.

BUCKS COUNTY RIVER COUNTRY

If you think tubing on the Delaware River includes dodging barges under the Ben Franklin Bridge, think again. Up north there's a kinder, gentler, and smaller stretch of river where the only thing you have to avoid is a sunburn. This is the province of BCRC, a tight ship of a watercraft-rental outfit, which shuttles hordes of river travelers—3,500 on a hot summer day—to drop-off points, from which they float or paddle down.

It's a relaxing way to spend a day. The river flows at a leisurely 1½ miles an hour, hovering at about 80°F in summer, and remaining clear and shallow (generally no more than 4 feet deep). Needing only slightly more muscle than couch potatoes, tubers range from infants (aboard parents) to ninetysomethings, and even those wary of water can't help but enjoy themselves.

Rentals entitle you to use the craft for the day. Tubers can opt to be dropped 3, 4½, or 6 miles upstream for a roughly 2-, 3-, or 4-hour drift. Rafts, canoes, and kayaks all leave

EATS FOR KIDS   Though boaters can bring food, tubers can't; it's too likely you'll lose your lunch overboard, literally. Because of strict rules about drinks on the river, thermoses (your own or rented) must be filled here. A unique alternative, the friendly **River Hot Dog Man** (Adventure Island, tel. 215/364–1193) sells hot dogs, burgers, kids' meals—even birthday cake, if you call ahead—from a midriver island. Prices aren't the cheapest, but you can't beat the location. The **Riverside Cafe,** a snack shack at BCRC, serves fast food and ice cream, as does **Dilly's Corner** (Rtes. 263 and 32, Center Bridge, tel. 215/862–5333).

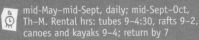

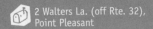 2 Walters La. (off Rte. 32), Point Pleasant

 215/297-5000

 Tubes $15 M–F, $17 Sa–Su; rafts $17–$20 per person; canoes $20–$25 per person; kayaks $25–$30 per person

mid-May–mid-Sept, daily; mid-Sept–Oct, Th–M. Rental hrs: tubes 9–4:30, rafts 9–2, canoes and kayaks 9–4; return by 7

 All ages

from the 6-mile spot, New Life Island, but canoes and kayaks generally travel twice as fast as tubes (assuming you paddle). Why hurry, though? The scenery—river islands, tree-covered shores, cliffs, and some houses, with the occasional jumping fish or soaring hawk for company—makes for a pretty float. Even on busy summer weekends, the river doesn't feel crowded.

Since there's no time limit on your trip (save for getting back by 7), feel free to stop for a swim from one of the lower islands. (The northern islands, occupied by a club and boy scout camp, are off-limits.) But make sure all kids wear life preservers. Follow the map printed on the tubes (on paper for boaters) to decide which sides of islands to navigate. There are some little rapids worth seeking out, or avoiding, depending on your inclination. The only thing you really need to remember, however, is not to get so relaxed that you miss the landing.

HEY, KIDS! You may be tempted to take something to do on your tube ride. Don't! For one thing, you'd miss the cool scenery. For another, you might lose something. People are always dropping things overboard.

KEEP IN MIND Costs for a day on the river can add up. There are extra charges for parking ($3), key storage ($1), and even a couple of bucks for rope to tie your family's tubes together (a good idea, so be sure to bring your own). Look for BCRC coupons, typically $2–$5 off, in newspapers or on the internet (www.rivercountry.net), including one for an early-bird special, if you come before 9:30. You can also ask the parking attendant about any discounts for the River Hot Dog Man, or check the web site (www.riverhotdogman.com).

CHANTICLEER

On 31 acres of hilly terrain lies a pleasure garden as opulent as its Main Line address. This was the country home of the Rosengarten family, and at one time three houses stood here, including those for children Adolph Jr. and Emily. But though Chanticleer (the main house) is open on guided tours, the grounds take center stage. Circling the estate, you pass from one act of a drama to another, from one carefully choreographed garden to the next. Flowers burst forth in almost gaudy profusion in spots, in creative understatement in others. And as befits a place where money seems to be of little object, it is the unexpected details that will likely capture your and your children's attention.

Start at the admission desk by Emily's house (now the administration building), and pick up a free Chanticleer book as lush as the gardens themselves. You'll have an inkling of what's to come as you pass a gorgeous handcrafted bench—woodworking here is a focus in itself—and enter the Tropical Teacup garden, showily abloom with exotic varieties. At the main house, a terrace overlooking a sloping lawn has two beautiful stone-inlaid

EATS FOR KIDS The **Villanova Diner** (797 E. Lancaster Ave., Villanova, tel. 610/527–9009) is at the U.S. 30/Rte. 320 intersection. **Bertucci's** (523 W. Lancaster Ave., tel. 610/293–1700) serves brick-oven pizza and pasta, and amuses kids with chalkboards and dough. Tidy picnicking is permitted at Chanticleer.

GETTING THERE From the Blue Route (I–476), take Exit 5 (Villanova). Take U.S. 30 east a few blocks; then turn right on Route 320 south. At the first light, turn right on Conestoga Road, and at the second light (Church Road), turn left. Chanticleer is ½ mile ahead on the right. If you'd rather go through Wayne, perhaps to get a bite to eat at one of its many restaurants, take U.S. 30 west (Lancaster Avenue) into town. Then to reach Chanticleer, take South Aberdeen Road (south), which winds through a residential area and turns into Church Road.

 786 Church Rd., Wayne

 610/687-4163

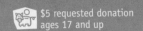 $5 requested donation
ages 17 and up

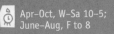 Apr–Oct, W–Sa 10–5;
June–Aug, F to 8

 All ages

rockers that positively call out to parents. Next to the chairs is a stroke of genius: bubble soap containers that call out equally to children. Behind Chanticleer, you can admire the plantings or the slate-lined pool with lion's-head fountain while your kids play a quick game of croquet on the manicured lawn.

For a change of pace, wander up the wavy lane between beds of grains and wildflowers penned in by junipers and culminating in a semicircle of Stonehenge-like pillars. Children uninterested in exploring every unusual nook and cranny can rest in the shade in a leopard-spot Adirondack chair.

Past woodland and water gardens, you arrive at the Ruin Garden, created when Adolph Jr.'s house was partially torn down in 1999. Here again beautiful materials, creative landscaping, and an imagination gone wild leave a wealth for big and little eyes to discover.

HEY, KIDS! Some of the most wonderful details at Chanticleer are the stones carved to look like something else. Can you find the rocks that look like a leaf fallen into a stream, a sleeping face, acorns, books? One of the books has acknowledgments reading, "Thanks Flora." Do you know what that means? Acknowledgments are the page in a book where the author gets to thank people. Flora is both a woman's name and a word meaning "plant life." In fact, you'll see several references to "Flora" around this garden brimming with plant life.

CHILDVENTURE

You're planning a camping trip. First you go to the grocery store and buy all sorts of healthy food. Next you make sandwiches with bread, cheese, and cold cuts. Finally, you head out to a campground in the woods and enter your tent, only to find an enormous bear and other woodland creatures awaiting your arrival. These are the experiences in store for your kids in just the first room of this compact children's play space.

The Childventure Museum and Shop is indeed a small place for small people. Unfortunately, you enter straight into the shop portion, but from there it's on to several tidy rooms of nonstop fun. The aforementioned combination Main Street/campground room also includes CV's Hardware and the Soda and Sandwich Shop to fuel those pretend-play muscles. Don't worry: Tools and food are plastic and completely safe for the under-3 set, and everything here is cleaned regularly. In addition, you'll find rooms for climbing and sliding, playing musical instruments (mostly percussion), and sitting somewhat quietly and

KEEP IN MIND Costumes in the storybook room are easy for little ones to put on (they close with Velcro)—so easy, in fact, that many a parent has donned attire, especially to coax an anxious toddler. Please keep track of your children's clothes, not to mention your children. Once upon a time, a group left behind all sorts of apparel, including a dress. Parents are asked to help youngsters return the costumes, and indeed all of the toys, to their rightful place, so that Childventure can stay neat and tidy—and hopefully kids will learn good habits.

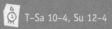
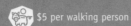

watching a simple slide show to music. Make-believe takes flight again in the storybook room, whose theme (e.g., Camelot, the Wizard of Oz, the circus) changes from year to year. The space always has books, costumes, and props, so children can play whatever role suits them at the moment and then—presto—change into something else. An exhibit room, in back, is the only other room that is completely changed annually, though it always maintains a cultural emphasis.

Most families stay about 1½ hours, though some have been known to stay all day, especially a rainy day. That can get hard on parents, who will eventually notice the absence of grown-up seating. The reason for this is that Childventure aims to foster interactive play, parents included. So bring your children and your inner child, and be prepared to get down and not dirty at all.

GETTING THERE Take Route 309 or the Pennsylvania Turnpike to Fort Washington. Proceed up Pennsylvania Avenue to the first light (Commerce Drive), and turn right. At the first stop sign, turn right again. Childventure is the third building on your left, en route to the Expo Center.

EATS FOR KIDS Though no food is allowed in the museum, you can have lunch at any of several local eateries and return later—even after a nap—since admission is for the whole day. Just down the street, **Mama's Pizza** (1704 Susquehanna Rd., Dresher, tel. 215/540–8280) serves great pies, including cheese steak pizza, barbecue pizza, primavera vegetable pizza, and baked ziti pizza, along with plain old cheese for those traditionalist tots. Not far in the other direction, you'll find tried-and-true **Friendly's** (325 Pennsylvania Ave., tel. 215/646–1944).

CHINATOWN

A few blocks north of Market Street, Philadelphia's Chinatown may not be as well-known or as large as San Francisco's or New York's, but it, too, is an oasis of Chinese culture in the middle of a modern American city. Just walking around and absorbing the culture is an eye-opening experience for kids. They might notice that stores and restaurants are both similar to and different from the ones they're used to, that most people are speaking Chinese rather than English, and that signs are written in both languages.

In fact, one of the first things you'll notice is that Chinatown's street signs are bilingual—that is, unless you enter via 10th Street. As you cross Arch Street, you'll notice instead an arch—the Chinese Friendship Gate, to be exact. This ornate 40-foot-tall arch was made by Chinese artisans with materials donated by Philadelphia's sister city in China, Tianjin. More Chinese flavor comes courtesy of pagoda-topped telephone booths and Chinese characters in the sidewalks.

KEEP IN MIND In addition to owning an Asian fusion restaurant, Joseph Poon (1002 Arch St., tel. 215/928–9333) is a skilled Chinatown interpreter. He leads tours, often on Sunday mornings, tied in with a meal at his restaurant. Call ahead to make arrangements.

EATS FOR KIDS With more than 50 restaurants to choose from, it's hard to choose one. But no visit to Chinatown would be complete without your doing just that. Order something not found at your local Chinese restaurant, and try eating with chopsticks. After all, when in Rome (or in this case, Beijing)... Some choices include **David's Mai Lai Wah Restaurant & Noodle House** (1001 Race St., tel. 215/627–2610), **Joe's Peking Duck House** (925 Race St., tel. 215/922–3277), and **H.K. Golden Phoenix Restaurant** (911–913 Race St., tel. 215/629–4988), outside which you'll find a plaque commemorating Chinatown's birthplace.

 Between 9th and 11th Sts., Arch and Vine Sts.

 Free

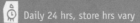 Daily 24 hrs, store hrs vary

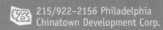 215/922–2156 Philadelphia Chinatown Development Corp.

 5 and up

Stroll the streets and explore the stores. Gift shops redolent with incense sell everything from souvenir carvings to Pokémon toys, from bamboo stalks to ginseng in various forms. Kids like Asia Crafts (123 N. 10th St.), which sells Japanese and Chinese imports. Equally alluring are the food stores, such as Chung May (1017 Race St.), a Chinese grocery. Where fish are sold, you won't just find them on ice; you'll see tanks of eels, lobsters, and fish whose names you don't know, waiting to become tonight's dinner.

Signs for acupuncturists, Chinese video rentals, and herbalists are interspersed with those for travel agents and cell phone stores. This is a working community, after all. And naturally there are Chinese restaurants, over 50 in total. At the Chinese Cookie Factory (155 N. 9th St., tel. 215/922–7288), you can buy a bag of fortune cookies or, if you're lucky, peek behind the counter. Here a mixer blends batter, while machines suck it up and turn it into that famous Chinese restaurant dessert—a fitting end to a Chinatown visit.

GETTING THERE Chinatown streets are busy, and what with the convention center nearby, traffic can get snarled, and street parking is tough to find. Lots are available, but they're not cheap. It's easier just to take public transportation, even if you're coming from outside the city, since the Market East station is just a few blocks away. And because Chinatown is so close (within 10 blocks) to most of the Center City and Old City sights in this book, it makes a great and filling place to end a day spent elsewhere.

CITY HALL

It's impressive. This immense French Second Empire–style edifice, which took 30 years to build in the late 19th century, was supposed to be the world's tallest building. Though surpassed by the Eiffel Tower and the Washington Monument by the time of its completion, it was still the tallest functional building for several years and today remains the largest U.S. city hall and the world's biggest all-masonry building. Even more impressive is that kids are actually interested in it. Depending on age and inclination, they may marvel at the sculpture (over 250 figures by Alexander Milne Calder) or the scale (88 million bricks used), at the remarkable circular staircases made of cantilevered granite, or at the beautiful view from the tower, nearly 500 feet up.

Kids who've learned about Pennsylvania or Philadelphia history or who understand the basics of government might enjoy taking one of the 90-minute public tours, which you can leave at any time. Volunteer guides from the Foundation for Architecture escort you to executive, legislative, and judicial areas within the massive structure, but thankfully to only a

HEY, KIDS! William Penn, a Quaker, founded Pennsylvania as a colony where people could worship freely. At the center of his plan for Philadelphia ("the City of Brotherly Love") was a square now occupied by City Hall, so it's appropriate that Penn himself stands atop its tower. From the observation deck, you see him overhead. He's 37 feet high—the tallest statue on any building in the world—and his 5-foot feet and hands might be longer than you. To grasp how big Billy is, check out the photo in the Tower Exhibit Room, and compare him to a real person.

Broad and Market Sts., tour office Room 121

 Free

215/686-1776, 215/686-2840 tours

 Tours M–F 12:30, tower M–F 9:30–4:30

Tours 10 and up, tower 5 and up

fraction of the nearly 700 rooms. You might see the mahogany-paneled Mayor's Reception Room, with its portraits of former mayors; the marble and Tiffany-glass-decorated City Council Meeting Room, where laws are passed; and the Supreme Court. Restoration of the exterior to its original grandeur is under way.

Younger children enjoy following the red lines on the seventh floor and taking the cramped elevator to the tower. (The elevator may be a bigger problem for claustrophobes than the enclosed observation area is for acrophobes.) Until the 1980s, this was the highest spot in Philadelphia, and though it can't compare to modern skyscraper observation decks in other cities, it still offers a nice panorama. Pick up the "Philadelphia City Hall Tower Views" pamphlet from either the tour office or the desk at the elevator entrance, and see which landmarks you recognize. Or just gaze down at what seem like Matchbox cars, and enjoy a quiet perch above the hubbub.

EATS FOR KIDS

Try a Billypop, an appropriately shaped lollipop, on sale in the tour office. For more substantial fare and rock-theme decor, head to the **Hard Rock Cafe** (12th and Market Sts., tel. 215/238–1000) or the **Reading Terminal Market** (*see* Pennsylvania Academy of the Fine Arts).

KEEP IN MIND Access to the tower is first-come, first-served. Please note, though, that mornings tend to be reserved for groups and 2–2:45 is saved for the public tour. Visitors on the tour stay in the tower only 5–8 minutes; visitors at other times can stay a little longer. On crowded summer days or holidays, timed tickets are issued, so you can do something else for a while and come back at your appointed slot. Be warned, though, that on the busiest days, tickets might all be gone by 3. Of course, be sure to come on a clear day.

CRAYOLA FACTORY

Don't drive here expecting to tour the real Crayola factory, which is actually outside town. What you'll find instead is a cheerfully colored kid's attraction including a small area devoted to demonstrations of crayon- and marker-making and many other areas devoted to creativity and fun.

The undisputed highlight is the manufacturing area, where amusing staff demonstrate and describe crayon production. (Bet you didn't know that over 130 billion Crayola crayons have been made since 1903 or that annual U.S. production would circle the globe 4½ times.) Watch through windows as melted wax is poured into a molding table, and, upon cooling, emerges as 1,200 brand-new crayons. They're labeled, boxed, and put in a dispenser, where you can buy them with tokens you receive with admission. A similar marker demonstration and dispenser are here, too. Strategically placed mirrors let even small-fry see what's happening, albeit upside down.

HEY, KIDS!
Check out Inside Out, two curving walls of glass that you can draw on with markers. Practice "mirror writing" and see if someone on the other side of the wall can read it. Play ticktacktoe through glass. Or just express yourself however you want—clearly!

KEEP IN MIND
Though the fastest routes here involve the Northeast Extension and I–78, consider taking back roads through beautiful Bucks County. Scenic stretches, like Routes 611 and 32 (avoid on crowded summer weekends), can also take you to other worthwhile sights. Ringing Rocks Park (Ringing Rocks Rd., off Rte. 32 and Bridgeton Hill Rd., Upper Black Eddy, tel. 215/757–0571) contains a field of boulders that can be "rung" with a hammer—be sure to bring one. Also in a geologic vein, Lost River Caverns (726 Durham St., Hellertown, tel. 610/838–8767) has chambers with crystal formations and an underground stream.

 Two Rivers Landing,
30 Centre Sq., Easton

 $8 ages 3 and up

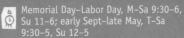 Memorial Day–Labor Day, M–Sa 9:30–6,
Su 11–6; early Sept–late May, T–Sa
9:30–5, Su 12–5

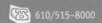 610/515-8000

 2–12

The rest of the "factory" is for hands-on expression, with plenty of Crayola products—and helpful staff—at everyone's disposal. Be prepared to leave toting a bag of masterpieces. Themes change monthly in the three main areas: Super Sculptures has modeling-clay projects, Easton Press & Bindery showcases printing, while the Creative Studio encourages free-form creativity, with liberal use of glue sticks. Other areas range from a color-your-own-slide room to a blackboard sidewalk to the Color Garden, where tots 5 and under can sort plastic fruit to their hearts' content. Sinks are at the ready for craft-encrusted hands. Also included is admission to the third-floor National Canal Museum, a quiet retreat but probably of less interest to most youngsters.

So, when all is said and done, is it worth driving 1½ hours to draw and stick and stamp and mold? The answer is yes. Frankly, sitting down to color at an immense spinnable crayon carousel has an allure that sitting at home with a box of 64 just doesn't. The only time kids seem sad here is when parents try to take them home.

EATS FOR KIDS Though the **McDonald's Express** (tel. 610/258-9603) in the building is the most obvious and convenient choice, it's not necessarily the best. Centre Square and adjacent streets offer quite a few alternatives. **Josie's New York Deli** (14 Centre Sq., tel. 610/252-5081) sells good-size deli sandwiches for under $3. Eat inside or, on a nice day, in the pretty fountain-centered park in the square. The **Easton Sweet Shop** (251 Centre Sq., tel. 610/252-3672) takes you back to the heyday of the luncheonette; it serves burgers, cheese steaks, and daily specials with soup.

Like other such institutions, this small museum has a whole lot of taxidermy going on. There's a big stuffed polar bear, a Delaware stream diorama with an otter posed as if it's fishing, and an African waterhole scene with a secretary bird, dik-dik, and gnu. The problem is, parents might not think these scenes seem "gnu" at all. To kids, however, it hardly matters. At first sight of the warthog, many erupt in squeals of "Pumbaa," and the rest, as they say, is history—natural history, that is.

The museum is more than stuffed animals, however, though even parents might find the bird dioramas in convex globes unusual and a display on the taxidermy process informative. If you like shells, you'll love the exhibit here, with examples ranging from pea-size faucet snails—so named because they clogged faucets in the 1890s—to a giant clam, the world's largest shelled mollusk. Other highlights include a simulated coral reef in the floor (you actually walk over it) and a wall of eggs. A short movie near the waterhole gives you a chance to sit down. And what natural history museum would be complete without dinosaur skeletons?

HEY, KIDS! Want to impress people with your knowledge of dinosaurs? The two skeletons here are both from China in the late Jurassic period. That's 150 million years ago, give or take a few million years. The two-footed one was a meat-eater named Yangchuanosaurus. The four-footed one was a plant-eater named Tuojiangosaurus. If you really want to impress someone, try saying those names three times fast.

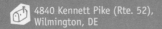
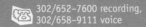
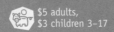

But perhaps the section likely to engage youngsters the longest is the Discovery Room. In this hands-on space, kids play with all sorts of games and puzzles. Children can answer questions about natural objects from the moderately hard (Whose home was this? A paper wasp's) to the easy (Who chewed this piece of wood? A beaver, natch). There are even lockers of clothes children can try on to transform themselves into all sorts of -ologists: a marine biologist (watch those swim fins), an entomologist, a paleontologist, and a forest ranger.

Though the Delaware museum isn't as big as the Academy of Natural Sciences (*see above*), it does offer something its city cousin doesn't: outside space. If the weather cooperates, end your visit with a trip to the outdoor butterfly house or take a walk on one of the trails and see the natural world before it's history.

GETTING THERE Despite its address, the museum is actually closer to Pennsylvania than to the city of Wilmington. Take I-95 south to Exit 3. Follow U.S. 322 west for 7 miles, U.S. 1 south for 8 miles, and Route 52 south for 5 miles. The museum is on your right.

EATS FOR KIDS The **Charcoal Pit** (2600 Concord Pike [U.S. 202], tel. 302/478-2165) serves very good hamburgers along with things that go very well with them: fries, shakes, and sundaes. Going into Greenville on Route 52 brings you to a number of good eating options, including **Pizza by Elizabeth** (4019 Kennett Pike, tel. 302/654-4478), which serves gourmet (e.g., topped with spicy cream cheese and roasted chicken) and nongourmet pizza, as well as BrewHaHa and the Brandywine Brewing Company and Restaurant (*see* Hagley Museum).

DORNEY PARK AND WILDWATER KINGDOM

Only five flags fly atop the entrance booth when you drive in, but there's nothing lacking at this clean, well-maintained, and manageable amusement and water park. A handful of thrill coasters coupled with classic rides and copious water slides make this a reasonably priced way to spend a full day.

Towering above Dorney is the Dominator, which takes you on a precipitous and unexpected plunge or launch (your choice), forcing your stomach into your throat (or vice versa) and making you wonder if the first letter of the ride's name is wrong. The coasters are the huge, fast Steel Force; loopy Laser; Hercules, a big wooden hulk; the smaller, vintage wooden Thunderhawk; the dipping, zigzagging Wild Mouse; and the new four-inversion Talon. Less thrilling rides abound, too, and (for the littlest visitors) thoughtful touches help. Thrill ratings (1–5) go height restrictions one better, keeping you from misjudging what you're getting into. Parents with an under-height child can do a parent swap, so each parent can ride without waiting in line twice. Alternatively, you can usually find a nearby

GETTING THERE
Access is easy from I–78 east (Exit 16) or west (Exit 16B) or the Northeast Extension (Exit 33) via Route 22 east to Route 309/I–78 east. Exit 16 puts you on Hamilton Boulevard; 16B necessitates a left turn. Then turn left on Lincoln Avenue to Dorney.

KEEP IN MIND
Changing clothes and shoes could be the trickiest part of your day. First, get a locker; it'll cost either $1 each time you open it (near the entrance) or $4 or $6 for the day, depending on size (Wildwater Kingdom). All Dorney rides except White Water Landing and Thunder Canyon require street clothes and shoes. Don't go barefoot on Thunder Canyon, though, as you have to traverse a long metal grating. Wildwater Kingdom rides require swimsuits and bare feet or water shoes (no sport sandals), and though water shoes are sold here, it's at a premium. Better to come prepared.

 3830 Dorney Park Rd., Allentown

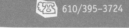 610/395-3724

 48" or taller: early–late May $19, late May–late June and late Aug–mid-Sept $26, late June–late Aug $33.50; $12 ages 4 and up but under 48" in shoes

 Hrs vary by season; heart of the summer generally 10–10, with Wildwater Kingdom closing at 8

 2 and up

kiddie ride, like the Little Laser, so you won't have to stand around or hike to Camp Snoopy, while waiting for thrill-seeking relatives.

Two more "thunders" on the supposedly dry Dorney side are Thunder Canyon, a wet raft trip, and the Thunder Creek Mountain log flume. But the flume's final splash can't touch White Water Landing in speed or water volume. Standing on the bridge at the bottom gets you drenched.

Where there's thunder there must be lightning: Wildwater Kingdom's Lightning Falls, that is. This is just one of the rides (many with alliterative names, like Riptide Run, Speed Slides, and Torpedo Tube) that plunge you down chutes of water—with tubes or without, twisty or straight, in light or darkness. Before settling on a favorite, tube the river floats and wade into the wave pool, with 10 minutes of waves followed by 10 minutes of calm. It's probably the closest to calm you'll get all day.

EATS FOR KIDS Not surprisingly, the top tier of the food pyramid is well represented at Dorney concessions. You'll find **Subway, Taco Bell, Burger Barn,** and purveyors of pizza, hot dogs, cheese steaks, and funnel cakes, along with the sit-down, air-conditioned **Red Garter Saloon** and **Coasters Drive-In.** Away from the park, **T.G.I. Friday's** (395 S. Cedar Crest Blvd., at Hamilton Blvd., tel. 610/776–8188) serves the chain's usual dependable fare and crayons. Other chains, such as Boston Market, Perkins, and Outback Steakhouse, are also in the vicinity.

EASTERN STATE PENITENTIARY

Y ou might think time-outs are a recent development in behavior modification. Truth is, Philadelphia prison reformers beat modern child-rearing experts by nearly 200 years. Back in the early 19th century, a group influenced by Quaker thought developed the radical idea that instead of floggings and other corporal punishment, what criminals really needed was complete isolation so they could reflect on their offenses and reform. The result was Eastern State Penitentiary, which cost nearly $800,000 to build—an immense amount at the time—and served as a prison for 142 years.

Enter the imposing castle-like structure and don a hard hat for a guided tour. Ghostly corridors and crumbling cells resonate with the memories of the men, women, and children who served time here. Tours run chronologically, starting with the oldest cell block (1829) and ending by death row, which was state-of-the-art in 1957. (The prison finally closed in 1971.) Early prisoners lived in 8-foot-by-12-foot cells. They had no way to communicate or even see one another, nothing to read or do (bibles and work were privileges to be

HEY, KIDS! Penal institutions have different names. ("Penal," as in the word "penalty," means having to do with punishment.) Jails usually hold people after their arrest and before or during trial. Once they're convicted, criminals go to prisons, sometimes called penitentiaries. "Penitentiary," which contains the word "penitent" (meaning sorry for what you've done), implies that the institution's purpose isn't just to punish criminals or to keep them away from regular citizens, but to get them to repent. Early sentences at Eastern State were shorter than today's—two or three years on average, 15 at most—because by then the prisoners should have reformed.

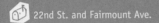 22nd St. and Fairmount Ave.

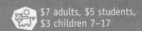 $7 adults, $5 students, $3 children 7–17

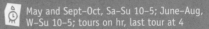 May and Sept–Oct, Sa–Su 10–5; June–Aug, W–Su 10–5; tours on hr, last tour at 4

 215/236–3300

 7 and up (minimum: 5)

earned down the line), and few diversions, save two daily half-hour sessions in tiny private exercise yards. Some inmates actually tamed birds or mice to have some interaction. By 1913, solitary confinement was abandoned and the penitentiary was converted for congregate use.

Tour guides happily answer questions, and kids seem particularly interested in such details of daily life as the toilets, which were connected to a pipe that was centrally flushed once a day. (Note that at the same time, in the 1820s, the White House still had an outhouse.) Guides also recount tales of the prison's infamous residents, among them bank robber Willie Sutton, who in 1945 escaped through a tunnel with 11 other inmates only to be recaptured a few minutes later, and Al Capone, who spent eight months here in 1929–30. After your tour, check out his cushy cell, with antiques and an Oriental rug—it's not exactly what those early prison reformers had in mind.

EATS FOR KIDS
Fairmount Pizzeria (2000 Fairmount Ave., tel. 215/763–1985) turns out big, thick, tangy pizza. Think twice before ordering two slices. Though fancier, **London Grill** (2301 Fairmount Ave., tel. 215/978–4545) still welcomes children, offering a kids' menu and child portions of regular menu items.

KEEP IN MIND Come October, the prison transforms nightly into a haunted "big house" for a Halloween extravaganza that is decidedly uneducational and unhistorical. (Regular daytime tours are still offered.) High-tech lighting and sound, props, animatronics, and actors turn the already creepy space into something truly frightening, best for teens and other scare-seekers. However, during the first few hours on Sunday evenings—dubbed Slight Fright—the fright factor is turned down a notch for younger kids. Children who are too scared can say "Monster be good." See www.easternstate.org for details.

ELMWOOD PARK ZOO

With a major zoo right in Philadelphia, why come to this smaller suburban zoo dedicated to North American animals? The answer is simple—literally. The Elmwood Park Zoo is contained and manageable, admission is very affordable, and parking is both easy and free. For the youngest zoo visitors, the absence of enormous elephants and rare rhinos hardly matters. There are interesting animals aplenty in relatively naturalistic environments and even a barn full of farm friends ready to be petted.

Paved paths lead you past enclosures with jaguars and timber wolves, bald eagles and bighorn sheep. Kids watch delightedly as a coatimundi (a raccoon relative) walks upside down across the ceiling of its cage. Signs throughout offer up educational insights, such as that the turkey vulture's bald head isn't just for good looks, but rather for hygiene; you can never be too clean when dining on carrion or the occasional poached (stolen) egg.

GETTING THERE From the Pennsylvania Turnpike or Blue Route (I–476), take Germantown Pike west to U.S. 202 south, which makes a right turn onto Johnson Highway. Past the second light, turn left on Chain Street; the zoo is three blocks on your right. Call for directions from other locations.

HEY, KIDS! Keeping the cats here straight can be difficult. The smallest resident, the bobcat (a.k.a. wildcat) has cute tufts in its ears. Its neighbor, the bigger, dirty-brown cougars, go by the aliases puma, mountain lion, and catamount. Watch as they clean themselves and bat at each other—a lot like house cats—but these guys can pounce 20 feet to catch a deer. Down the hill, two jaguars look nothing alike. One is sleek and black, the other spotted, but don't confuse these Central and South American natives with leopards, which come from Asia and Africa. You wouldn't want to get these guys angry.

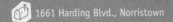
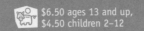
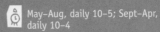

In the walk-through wetlands aviary, you actually enter the animals' cage and amble on a walkway above various ducks and geese. But the aviary's star is a ham of a river otter, who obliges the audience by rolling around on land, gracefully swimming in its waterfall-fed pond, and dancing (seemingly begging) on its hind feet. But don't even think of feeding it, or any animal here except for the barn animals and the outdoor ducks—corn dispenser provided.

Plans for a new prairie dog and black-footed ferret exhibit, call for domes for kids to pop up in to get a prairie-dog's-eye view. Conservation Kingdom, an interactive playground, opened in May 2001. These are just part of the continuing upgrades aimed at renewing this New World zoo.

EATS FOR KIDS A couple of picnic areas on zoo grounds are great places to enjoy a packed lunch or one bought at the **Cougar Cafe** (weekends only in winter), which cooks up chicken nuggets and hot dogs and sells that all-important ice cream. Farther into the zoo, the **Jaguar Juice Bar** (closed winter) sells only drinks and snacks, including icy treats. Off zoo premises, there isn't much. **Via Veneto Pizza** (1803 Markley St., tel. 610/279–5222) and **Rita's Water Ice** (1727 Markley St., tel. 610/292–8575) are good places for their eponymous eats.

FAIRMOUNT PARK

Philadelphia has an enormous backyard—Fairmount Park—filled with things to do. Most park descriptions discuss historic mansions and vestiges of the Centennial Exposition of 1876. These are okay, but do your kids a favor and leave the history lesson at home.

The park's best-known sections flank the Schuylkill River. In the East Park, bladers and bikers, walkers and joggers throng to Kelly Drive, especially along Boathouse Row, home to many local rowing clubs. (The drive's mirror image, West River Drive, is closed to cars on weekends April to October and so also draws an active crowd.) Take a family outing and watch the crews rowing on the river. Up the hill near the reservoir is a landmark as revered as any in Philly: the giant indoor slide at the Smith Memorial Playground and Playhouse, not to be confused with the Smith Memorial, in the West Park. The playhouse is a three-story, toy-filled playroom that's like a day-care center open to the public. The adjacent playground is dotted with older metal equipment and its share of urban litter,

KEEP IN MIND According to the Fairmount Park Commission, no city resident lives more than a mile from a park in the 8,700-acre Fairmount Park system, which, by the way, is larger than some foreign countries. Its tentacles spread from Pennypack Park, in Northeast Philadelphia, to the Wissahickon gorge (*see below*) to FDR Park, home to the city's skateboard park (closes at 9) near the sports complex in South Philly. Philadelphia Trolley Works (*see below*) operates a separate park trolley that makes about five stops in either the East or West Park. The route changes daily, so inquire before boarding.

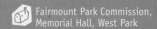
Fairmount Park Commission, Memorial Hall, West Park

215/685–0000 FPC, 215/878–5097 Japanese House

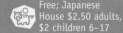
Free; Japanese House $2.50 adults, $2 children 6–17

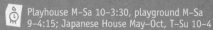
Playhouse M–Sa 10–3:30, playground M–Sa 9–4:15; Japanese House May–Oct, T–Su 10–4

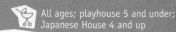
All ages; playhouse 5 and under; Japanese House 4 and up

but its centerpiece is a green shed that children and parents (perhaps when they were kids, too) have visited for over 80 years. Inside, a waxed-daily wooden slide is wide enough for a small scout troop to slide down side by side. Grab a burlap sack before ascending—you'll go faster and stay cleaner—and come down forwards, backwards, sideways, or even surf-ways (but be careful!).

For a marked contrast, visit the West Park's Japanese House. Modeled on a 17th-century palatial home, the graceful building sits beside a water garden. Admission includes a 30- to 45-minute guided tour that many kids enjoy, perhaps because the house is so different from their own ("Where's the bed?"). They especially like taking off their shoes before entering, practicing Japanese words, and visiting the small teahouse with its low ceiling. Below the Japanese House, a small trail leads into the woods to a pavilion in the treetops. You'd never guess you were in the big city's backyard.

HEY, KIDS! Attention music-lovers: The Mann Center for the Performing Arts (West Park, tel. 215/546–7900) offers free kids' concerts on a handful of weekday mornings in July and August. Concerts might range from the Philadelphia Orchestra to jazz, musical theater to world rhythms.

EATS FOR KIDS A day in the park deserves a picnic. Picnic areas throughout the park include ones at the Belmont Plateau and Smith Playground, where a mini-store sells hot dogs. Or create an impromptu picnic in a lovely spot, such as the pavilion in the trees. Eat inside or out at the East Park's **Lloyd Hall** (1 Boathouse Row, Kelly Dr., tel. 215/685–3934), a recreation center with café. A truck often sells hot dogs and hamburgers outside. **Parlor on the Parkway** (2601 Pennsylvania Ave., tel. 215/684–0314) is an ice cream parlor/coffee bar serving sandwiches, salads, and baked goods, too.

FIREMAN'S HALL

What kid doesn't love fire trucks? Fireman's Hall, operated by the Philadelphia Fire Department, may not have the drama of a charging engine, but in its quiet way, the museum enchants would-be firefighters all the same.

Little guys (let's face it, firefighting is a guy thing, though girls might like the hall, too) gravitate to the shiny red vintage equipment—from a 1730 Richard Newsham hand engine (with a good tailwind, it could maybe shoot a stream 25 feet) to the 1896 LaFrance-Hayes Aerial Ladder to the 1903 Cannon Wagon, designed to deal with those newfangled "skyscrapers." Schoolkids can also appreciate the stories told here about the history of firefighting and the lives of nearly three centuries of Philadelphia firefighters.

Exhibits range from a re-created fireboat pilot house with movable wheel to a memorial to Philadelphia firemen killed in the line of duty—tragically, about two a year to this day. A display on the evolution of helmets explains why they have those big brims in

KEEP IN MIND While you're here, walk down Elfreth's Alley (Front to 2nd Sts. between Arch and Race Sts.), the country's oldest continually occupied residential street. Its brick row homes are privately owned, except for two, which re-create the homes of a Windsor chair maker and mantua maker (dressmaker).

EATS FOR KIDS To continue the firefighting experience, head down Columbus Boulevard to **Engine 46 Steak House** (10 Reed St., tel. 215/462–4646), in an old firehouse. Firefighting decor ranges from hydrants to dalmatian tablecloths, and a pole descends through a table for six. The firefighting theme extends even to the menu, which includes the fire drill fillet and four-alarm cheese fries (the specialty, naturally, is steak) along with standard kids' food. For someplace closer, try **Snow White Restaurant** (200 Market St., tel. 215/923–2342), which serves classic diner food a couple of blocks from the museum. Also see other Old City sights.

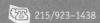 147 N. 2nd St.

 T–Sa 9–4:30, 1st F of mth to 9:30

Donations accepted

215/923–1438

2–12

back (to keep water off firefighters' necks) and aren't made of metal (so as not to conduct electricity). Speaking of electricity, Ben Franklin takes his customary place of honor as an organizer of the first volunteer fire department (1736) and the first successful fire insurance company, the Philadelphia Contributionship (1752). Interestingly, Franklin's company wouldn't insure homes with a tree nearby: Franklin knew about the dangers of lightning. But the Mutual Assurance Company would, as indicated by the tree on its fire mark. Fire marks, attached to houses, showed which company insured each house, serving both to advertise and to let fire companies know who would reimburse them for their efforts.

If you come to Fireman's Hall expecting flashing lights and sirens, bells and whistles—or even to climb on equipment or slide down a pole—you'll be disappointed. If you come expecting to learn about firefighting, you won't be. As befits an 1876 firehouse with a huge stained-glass mural of a firefighter rescuing a child, the hall is a shrine to this noble profession.

HEY, KIDS! Before there was modern communication and transportation, there was the Gamewell Joker and the horse. The Joker was the system that informed firehouses where a fire was. Brass gongs in every firehouse rang out a pattern representing a number (#1776 meant Independence Hall). It's said that some fire horses were smart enough to tell by the rings if the fire was in their district and they were about to go to work. They pulled heavy equipment to the scene and stood patiently, ignoring the smoke, sparks, and commotion. So they weren't just smart, but strong and brave, too.

FIRST UNION CENTER TOUR

Sports fans, don your favorite player's jersey for this behind-the-scenes tour of the arena that ice hockey's Flyers, basketball's 76ers, and lacrosse's Wings call home. If you're a First Union Center veteran, being in this huge building when it's so quiet and empty may seem strange, but having the place almost to yourself is part of the fun.

Much of what you see on the tour is what you'd see if you were here for a game. Circling the concourse, you'll pass Flyer and Sixer photo galleries; actual championship banners; the 76ers Zone and Flyers Experience, where you can briefly use touch-screen computers on team history; a display of hats thrown on the ice after Flyer hat tricks; and a window into the Comcast SportsNet studio, where, at other times, SportsRISE and SportsNITE are taped. If this was all there was to the tour, it would be a disappointment, since even some items that are available during a game, like the interactive goalie, are shut down.

The reason to take the tour, however, is to see things you can't normally see: Sitting in a

HEY, KIDS! Ever wonder how hockey rinks and basketball courts are made? It takes 10,000 gallons of deionized water, 300 gallons of paint, and two days to build the Flyers' ice for the season. So what happens when the Sixers play? In as little as two hours, a crew removes 156 sheets of hockey glass and the boards, covers the ice with an insulating layer called homasote, and assembles a 296-piece wood floor like a jigsaw puzzle. One Valentine's Day, 75 couples got married at a Sixers' halftime. It was supposed to be 76. Perhaps the last couple thought they'd be on the hockey rink and got cold feet.

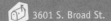 3601 S. Broad St.

 215/389–9543

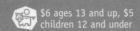 $6 ages 13 and up, $5 children 12 and under

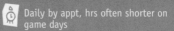 Daily by appt, hrs often shorter on game days

 6 and up

club box, you'll hear about the workings of the center and can ask your tour guide anything you want. (The most popular question is, "Has anyone ever fallen off the top level?" The answer, thankfully, is "no.") Then you'll go way up to that top, press-box level, 97 feet above the floor, and see what reporters see when they cover a game. On request, tours might visit Arenavision, where the huge video screens and speakers are controlled and where the organ is played. Time permitting, you might even see special images displayed on the Jumbotron.

For most fans, though, the biggest thrill is back down at floor level, when you look inside a Flyer and/or Sixer locker room and, if you're lucky, sit on the Flyers' bench or glimpse a visiting team practicing (the Flyers and Sixers have their own practice facilities). In fact, though tours are somewhat standard, you never know exactly what you'll see.

EATS FOR KIDS
The First Union Center's concessions and restaurants are closed at tour times. Local options include the **Riverview Deli** (Washington and Delaware Aves., tel. 215/334–4647) and, for Italian cuisine, **Medora's Mecca** (13th St. and Packer Ave., tel. 215/336–1655), which will make kids' portions.

KEEP IN MIND Call ahead to schedule a tour, and be flexible about times. Your family will probably join a preexisting group tour. Schedules, and what you'll see, vary based on events. So for example, if a trainer or team is using a locker room, you won't be able to visit it. If you really want to see a particular team's locker room, mention that when you reserve, so the schedule can be checked. Summer is a good time to tour, since facilities are more accessible; on the other hand, you won't see the court or rink (and thus can't warm the bench).

FONTHILL

Picture a child constructing rooms out of Legos or another building toy and then putting them together almost willy-nilly to make a castle. That's pretty much the process Henry Mercer (1856–1930) used to design Fonthill, the quirky home of this quirky but remarkable archaeologist turned Arts and Crafts–style tile-maker. Taking a tour of his mansion (all visits are by one-hour guided tour) may seem like just another house tour, but the building's unconventional aspects—and there are many—make it interesting even for kids.

What strikes you first is the building material—concrete—seemingly out of character for a man who, you'll learn, loved animals, nature, and the time-honored hand-craftsmanship expounded by the Arts and Crafts movement. But once you get inside and hear about Mercer, you'll understand that all is not so concrete. What at first seems cold and austere becomes a symbol of the straightforwardness of his vision and a perfect backdrop for displaying his tiles. Indeed tiles are the real star here. They adorn walls and floors, ceilings and columns. Most are Mercer's creations and are representational, depicting tales from

EATS FOR KIDS Have a picnic on the beautiful grounds or head to the **Cross Keys Diner** (4125 Swamp Rd., tel. 215/348–4911), whose sign proclaims "Good Eats." The little house doesn't look like anything, but the chili and sandwiches are really something. Also see the Mercer Museum.

KEEP IN MIND If the tiles at Henry's house intrigue you, visit his adjacent workshop. The Moravian Pottery & Tile Works (tel. 215/345–6722) is part tile factory, part living-history museum. Self-guided tours (every half hour) start with a historical video, which young children might fidget through. Then wander through the Spanish Mission–style concrete structure (warning: It can be hot in summer and cold in winter) and watch real ceramists making Mercer's original designs. The artisans happily answer questions while they stamp and press the red clay, which is transformed in six weeks from the raw clay of the dungeonlike clay pit to a finished tile.

E. Court St. and Rte. 313
(Swamp Rd.), Doylestown

215/348-9461

 $7 adults, $2.50
children 6–17

M–Sa 10–5, Su 12–5; last tour 4

8 and up

Bluebeard to Columbus-era cannibals. Others chronicle ceramic history, including Babylonian clay tablets dating to 2400 BC.

And then there's the curious layout. You could play hide-and-seek here for weeks on end, since rooms unfold one onto another, connected by strange little staircases—32 in all. Odd items of decor, such as the small stuffed alligator hanging in the Morning Room, add to the extraordinary feel.

Try to come the first Saturday of the month for a Tower Tour, designed specifically for families, though even the regular tour can interest children. Depending on available time and tour size (reservations are recommended, as the maximum is 12), guides try to involve kids, perhaps letting them make rubbings on the floor of the "saloon." If your children can view each room as an "I Spy" picture, with layer upon layer of detail to be patiently discovered, they can't help but be intrigued by all that's unusual here.

HEY, KIDS! Forget "Where's Waldo?" The game to play here is "Where's Rollo?" Of Henry Mercer's 12 Chesapeake Bay retrievers, loyal Rollo was his favorite. The dog was often at his master's side, even while Fonthill was being built. See if you can find evidence that this VIP (very important pet) set paw here. For a harder treasure hunt, look outside for another favorite Mercer animal: Lucy the horse. She and only 8 or 10 men built Fonthill and were each paid $1.75 per day; Lucy also got all the hay she could eat. You'll have to look up and down, literally, to find her.

FORT MIFFLIN

I n fall 1777, the British desperately needed to resupply their troops in Philadelphia so they could attack Gen. Washington before winter. Continental forces, however, held Fort Mifflin, on the Delaware River below the mouth of the Schuylkill. For seven weeks, the British laid siege to the fort, including six days constituting the heaviest bombardment of the Revolution. Finally, the determined Pennsylvania artillerists were forced to destroy and abandon the fort, having sustained a casualty rate of about 70%. But their valiant effort delayed the British long enough for the Continental Army to retreat to Valley Forge, probably preventing defeat. This is just one saga in the rich history of the (subsequently rebuilt) fort, which today makes for a peaceful outing despite the vestiges of war and the roar of jets from nearby Philadelphia International Airport.

Cross a moat lush with greenery and teeming with turtles, and walk through a big wooden door in thick brick walls. A 13-stripe Continental Navy flag flies above. In front of you, an array of yellow structures includes living quarters, a blacksmith's shop, an artillery shed,

HEY, KIDS! Oh, those darned flintlock muskets! Though used for over 200 years, they had their problems. One was that they took 15 to 20 seconds to load, requiring soldiers to stand close together, so some would be firing while others were reloading. Second, they were inaccurate. Last, they often misfired, maybe burning a soldier's beard, firing during loading (called "going off half-cocked"), or not firing when supposed to (like a "flash in the pan," when only the gunpowder in the pan, not the barrel, ignited). Plug your ears if you don't like loud noises, but don't miss the demonstration. It's a blast.

Fort Mifflin Rd. (off I–95 Exit 13)

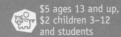 $5 ages 13 and up,
$2 children 3–12
and students

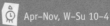 Apr–Nov, W–Su 10–4

215/685–4192

 3 and up

and torpedo and powder magazines. Before you start exploring, check the blackboard for times of tours and programs; you won't want to miss the uniform and weapons demonstration—not that you could, as the musket report is loud enough to be heard over a departing 747.

Kids like to enter, and scream in, the dark, thick-walled magazines. You'll wish you'd eaten more carrots here and in the casemates next to the main entrance. Built as bomb-proof rooms, these chambers later housed about 300 Civil War prisoners. Wander about and imagine yourself locked inside.

A reasonably comfy furnished junior officers' room stands in contrast to the soldiers' barracks, where five rooms housed 25 men each. Up on the sod-covered ramparts, you can walk the fort's circumference, keeping an eye peeled on the river and Center City—just in case an enemy appears.

KEEP IN MIND
Though the enclosed fort is a safe place for kids to romp, make sure their explorations are supervised. Don't climb over brick or slate walls or on the vegetation-covered magazines. And don't be scared by swallows, which can swoop out of buildings as you swoop in.

EATS FOR KIDS By far the best idea is to bring a packed lunch to eat in the shadow of the two big cannons at the Water Battery picnic area, just outside the moat. It's a lovely spot in which to enjoy the fort's wildlife, a very real bonus of a visit here. If you must get prepared food, you can eat at the **Landing Restaurant** (4500 Island Ave., tel. 215/937–4530), at the airport Hilton, or take your pick of a Burger King, Taco Bell, Pizza Hut, Wendy's, or Dunkin' Donuts up the road a ways at the **Penrose Plaza** (Island Ave.).

FRANKLIN COURT

Of all the sights in Independence National Historical Park (*see below*), Franklin Court is the most child-friendly. Consisting of the courtyard where Franklin's house and print shop once stood (suggested by modern steel "ghost structures") and an underground museum dedicated to the man, it offers special kids' programs and things for them to touch and work. That doesn't mean this is a state-of-the-art, hands-on place. It isn't. But Franklin Court does get kids out from behind velvet ropes and engaged in who Franklin was.

The spirit of '76 lives on here. Unfortunately, it's the spirit of 1976. Your first hint of "modernization" comes when you walk through the archway from Market Street and see the huge building outlines. Okay, you might reason, since there wasn't enough documentation to accurately reconstruct Franklin's house, better to give a modern interpretation, augmented by windows that peek below ground at pieces of original foundation. Downstairs in the museum, however, the modern touch loses some luster.

KEEP IN MIND Memorial Day to Labor Day from 10 to 12, you can meet Philadelphia's own Ben Franklin (Ralph Archbold) under the mulberry tree here. He makes an appearance with Washington at the Call to Arms, too (*see* Town Crier Summer Theatre).

EATS FOR KIDS Formica tables, 1950s–era vinyl chairs, and pressed-tin walls and ceiling set the vintage scene at the **Griffin Cafe** (230 Market St., tel. 215/ 829–1050). On the menu are cold and hot sandwiches, salads, and breakfast all day, including eggs and fillings rolled in a tortilla. Franklin Court's central Old City location puts it within a few blocks of all sorts of other eateries. See listings for the Arden Children's Theatre, Betsy Ross House, Fireman's Hall, Ghost Tour of Philadelphia, Independence National Historical Park, Lights of Liberty, Mum Puppettheatre, the National Liberty Museum, and the U.S. Mint.

Past an exhibit of period furnishings, you enter a room of inexplicable mirrors and flashing neon signs proclaiming "Scientist," "Statesman," "Author," and the like. Kids seem to like it, though it's questionable whether Ben would, his forward-thinking attitude notwithstanding. Next enter the Franklin Exchange, where rows of telephones stand on posts like a drive-in movie, and you can call famous people (listen for those pulse tones) to hear what they had to say about Franklin.

Though Franklin Court won't get a facelift until other park construction is complete, there's still plenty to enjoy. Watch the Discovery Channel movie *The Real Ben Franklin* or listen to a demonstration of the glass armonica, a Franklin-invented instrument played with fingers on the rims of glasses. Mail something at the post office on Market Street; it'll get a neat "B. Free Franklin" postmark. Through children's programs such as Hands on History, kids take part in journal writing, games, or playing a miniature glass armonica. It hardly matters that the museum hasn't changed much since before they were born.

HEY, KIDS! As you enter the courtyard from Market Street, look to the right. See those marble circles on the ground? One is inscribed, "Franklin Water Well, 1700s, 318 Market St.," while another, less than 10 feet away, reads, "Franklin Privy Pit, 1787, 318 Market St." Privy pits were where people disposed of—ahem—waste in those days. They didn't know about proper sanitation, the importance of clean water, and the spread of disease through germs. No wonder people were sicker back then!

FRANKLIN INSTITUTE

46

I t's fitting that in a city disposed to revere Ben Franklin, the institute of science and technology is named for him. After all, he's known as much for his inventions and scientific inquiry as for his role as a Founding Father. The most literal homage to Franklin is in the rotunda—a statue and artifacts that make up the only national memorial outside Washington, D.C.—but the real tribute is the museum itself. Like Franklin, the museum covers an eclectic mix of subjects, from electricity to weather, astronomy to anatomy. Like him, too, the museum is both venerable and forward-thinking. It maintains a dignified, long-established air while updating the technology of its exhibits to keep up with the technology of the times.

The Science Center has four floors of exhibits. (Those in the newer Mandell Center tend to be temporary traveling exhibits.) On the second floor, you'll find areas devoted to Franklin's amazing inventions and observations, especially those on electricity, and to bioscience, including the walk-through heart. Time hasn't changed kids' enjoyment of the giant organ,

KEEP IN MIND Early to bed, early to rise—Franklin's advice applies equally to preparing for a museum visit. You could easily spend a full day here, especially if you want to play outside in Science Park and watch an IMAX movie, a planetarium show (there's always one specifically for children, often around midday), and a show in the 3D Theater, which combines photography with laser images. Arriving early (and staying late) also gives you time in the exhibits without the big crowds, since the museum is as popular with school groups on weekdays as it is with families on weekends.

Benjamin Franklin Pkwy.
at 20th St.

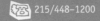 215/448-1200

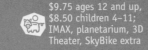 $9.75 ages 12 and up,
$8.50 children 4-11;
IMAX, planetarium, 3D
Theater, SkyBike extra

 Daily 9:30-5; IMAX films also F and Sa to
9; Science Park, Memorial Day-Labor Day,
daily 9:30-3, weather permitting

 5 and up

though the museum plans to update the exhibit around it, as it does for the beloved locomotive in the first floor's Railroad Hall.

One of the newest exhibits is the third floor's Sports Challenge, where virtual-reality and "challenge" games illustrate scientific principles. If Ben were here, he'd surely be a good sport and hop on the surfboard for the Balance Challenge or try Go with the Flow, a virtual-reality ski run that shows how body position affects speed. The new KidScience exhibit is designed for K–4 kids, the younger siblings of the museum's traditional 4th grade-and-up audience. The institute plans more changes in coming years. But regardless of how state-of-the-art exhibits are, from the new SkyBike, which hovers above the atrium on a cable (with a 250-pound counterweight that makes it stable), to Foucault's pendulum, which has been swinging in the stairwell since the museum opened in 1934, the scientific principles they reveal remain the same.

EATS FOR KIDS
Ben's Restaurant (tel. 215/448-1355), on the second floor, is a serviceable cafeteria. Also see suggestions for the Academy of Natural Sciences and Please Touch Museum.

HEY, KIDS! Many scientists and inventors besides Franklin are honored at the institute. One is Isaac Newton, a 17th-century mathematician and physicist who was a *very* smart guy. He'd probably have liked Newton's Dream—what the institute describes as a kinetic sculpture but really a gizmo with a lot of shooting, twisting, turning, spinning, and bouncing golf balls. Balls shoot into the air and then travel on rails down 10 different pathways. It's fun to try to predict which ways the balls will go and, if you get that intellectual curiosity going, to guess why they do what they do.

GARDEN STATE DISCOVERY MUSEUM

The name of this museum in a one-story suburban building tells a lot about what kind of place it is, but it doesn't explain everything. Even the word "Museum" might be misleading, since this isn't a look and learn from the exhibits kind of museum. It's a romp, build, touch, draw, hammer, dance, and climb on the exhibits kind of museum, a fact that contributes to the occasional section under repair. Kids don't seem to mind, though. They just play with something else.

The "Garden State" designation refers more to location than to subject matter, though some exhibits have a Jersey flair. At Down the Shore, your kids can climb in a lifeguard chair, sell ice cream from a cart, or scramble on the boat *Fish-N-Trips,* from which would-be anglers drop a line. At Inky's Newsroom, cub reporters can use a computer to compose their own story for the South Jersey edition of the *Inquirer*. Older kids generally write from scratch, while younger children can choose a pre-written article or create text by answering prompted questions. After having their picture taken,

KEEP IN MIND There's more to do here than simply play in the exhibits. Each month has a theme, and related performance-based events, complete with audience participation, are staged most weekends during the school year, weekdays in summer. Workshops for preschoolers (with parents) and young grade-schoolers (without) come in four-week sessions, and birthday parties make weekends busy. About twice a month on Saturday nights, the museum offers Parents' Night Out. For $20 for the first child (less each additional), your kids can enjoy three hours of food and fun at the museum while you can enjoy three hours of food and fun elsewhere.

16 N. Springdale Rd., Cherry Hill, NJ

 $6.95 ages 1 and up

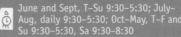 June and Sept, T–Su 9:30–5:30; July–Aug, daily 9:30–5:30; Oct–May, T–F and Su 9:30–5:30, Sa 9:30–8:30

 856/424–1233

 1–10

junior journalists retrieve their article, complete with byline and photo, from a printer concealed in a newspaper machine.

"Discovery" goes on at many levels here. Printed explanations impart information throughout, but for the most part, discovery results not from instruction but from imaginative play—in a treehouse or dog-grooming salon, on the rock-climbing wall or stage, or at the farm stand or Bubble Trouble exhibit. There's even a Little Discoveries area for preschoolers, so they can discover without getting bowled over by larger explorers. But one of the hottest spots is the Discovery Diner, where diminutive servers shuttle between booths full of customers and a kitchen full of cooks who give new meaning to the term "short order." Here you can watch news or weather telecasts from the museum's WPVI news desk, marvel at how much fun your kids have clearing the dishes, or rediscover how tasty plastic hamburgers can be.

EATS FOR KIDS Since man (woman, and child) cannot live by pretend pancakes alone, bring some real food and eat in the snack area (with vending machines) or in the Adventure Garden (May–October). Or have **Big John's** (tel. 856/424–1186) deliver pizza to the museum. At Springdale Plaza (Springdale and Greentree Rds.), choose from **Tao Yuan** (tel. 856/751–5111), for Chinese and Vietnamese fare, and **The Boyz** (tel. 856/751–3434), for subs and steaks. **Zac's Kitchen & Market** (12 Springdale Rd., tel. 856/489–7574) serves homemade soups, salads, and sandwiches.

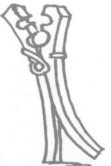

GHOST TOUR OF PHILADELPHIA

I t should come as no surprise that Philadelphia's most hallowed ground is also some of its most haunted, at least according to the folks who run this 1¼-hour candlelit ghost tour. The tour is like a movable campfire, where each stop brings another story. Whether or not you believe in ghosts, you should like the slightly spooky tales, woven into these historical surroundings.

You start in the shadow of Independence Hall, though depending on the time of year, there may be no shadows left. (Darkness does add to the atmosphere, but don't worry, it never feels truly scary.) Different guides embellish tales with different details and hypotheses, some a little more risqué than others, but all appropriate for schoolchildren.

Along the way, you'll hear about ghosts purportedly "seen" in Independence Hall, in adjacent Congress Hall, and in the nearby Library Hall—where you're told Ben Franklin himself has appeared. Throughout the tour, you're reminded that though the park service cannot

HEY, KIDS!   The best story is about the Hag of Pine Street. While standing in St. Peter's cemetery, you'll learn of this grouchy old snoop who hated noisy children and couples in love and who would stick her ugly, pale, wrinkled face against the window and bang her broom against the wall. It seems the neighborhood was waiting for her to die so she would stop interfering, which she eventually did—die, that is. But that didn't stop her from sticking her ugly, pale, wrinkled, dead face out the window and banging her broom. For the end of the story, you'll have to take the tour.

 5th and Chestnut Sts.

 $10 ages 13 and up, $5 children 3–12

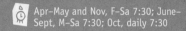 Apr–May and Nov, F–Sa 7:30; June–Sept, M–Sa 7:30; Oct, daily 7:30

 215/413–1997

 6 and up

confirm any sightings, some encounters were reported by security guards and rangers working in park buildings.

More stories unfold at Washington Square, which served as a sort of potter's field in the late 18th century, both for war dead and for victims of the yellow fever epidemic of 1793. The walk continues through the cobblestone streets of Society Hill to the graveyard outside St. Peter's Episcopal Church (where George Washington worshiped) and concludes behind the City Tavern after stops outside the Physick and Bishop White houses. Every stop has a ghost tale or two or three associated with it. You'll hear about caped men in tricorner hats, a wife driven mad, a cloaked figure with no face, a voodoo priest, spectral fogs, and even a bride-to-be killed on her wedding day. But we can't tell about them all here or it would spoil the fun.

EATS FOR KIDS
Tour tickets (advance phone reservations required) and a reasonably priced light dinner—e.g., hot and cold sandwiches, burgers, quiche—can both be purchased at **Willie & Duffy's** (620 Chestnut St., tel. 215/413–1744). For more options, see listings for Old City sights.

KEEP IN MIND At 7:30, on the southeast corner of 5th and Chestnut streets, you'll meet a dark stranger carrying a candle, but he or she won't be a stranger for long. That's your tour guide. Wear good walking shoes; you'll cover a lot of ground, some of it on cobblestone streets and brick sidewalks. In fact, it may be all the walking and waiting for red lights that keep the tour from getting scary—that and the cemetery's security light. The tales are pretty matter-of-fact, too, so you probably won't have to worry about nightmares...and your kids won't either.

GO VERTICAL

43

Okay, so a sea of tall pink, blue, green, and yellow stucco walls studded with small irregularly shaped, multicolor "rocks" and dangling ropes may not be the spitting image of El Capitan. Still, this large indoor rock-climbing gym just north of Penn's Landing is about the closest you'll come to climbing a peak in Philadelphia.

Like many climbing gyms, Go Vertical is primarily member-based, and indeed, part of the fun here is watching adept climbers scale the angular heights with agility and grace. Drop-in, first-time climbers can get a taste of the high by doing a "climb ride," an amusement experience that management created in recognition of the gym's urban location.

A climb ride consists of three climbs belayed by Go Vertical's professional staff. By being belayed—i.e., wearing a harness secured by a rope—you are completely safe. Required gear is included, though you're encouraged to wear sneakers. You don't need to know,

EATS FOR KIDS **Dave and Buster's** (325 N. Columbus Blvd., tel. 215/413–1951) has arcade games, billiards, and, oh yes, food. **Silk City Diner** (435 Spring Garden St., tel. 215/592–8838) serves good inexpensive fare, and **Wings to Go** (944 N. Delaware Ave., tel. 215/829–1100) has wings to stay, too.

KEEP IN MIND If you like the climb ride, the staff hopes you won't come back—to the climb ride, that is. The next step up is to take beginner classes that result in certification to belay and climb on your own. Adults take one class; teens must take two, but the class package includes two return passes to the gym. Upon completion, you can come climb anytime, paying only for a day pass and equipment rental, though eventually most people buy their own. From then on, you can belay for your kids and have them belay for you.

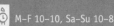
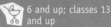
and won't learn, any rope-handling skills. All you have to remember is to wait until your belayer is ready. Then up you go, grabbing small hand- and footholds as you scale the 50-foot wall. If you poop out (this is strenuous stuff), feel free to stop, and your belayer will lower you gently back to terra firma. Or just pause, suspended above the action, until you're ready to proceed. Even people afraid of heights don't tend to have problems, since your focus is on what's above you.

The staff offers gentle help and encouragement, urging but not pressuring. Young kids might be reluctant to go very high on their first climb, not always realizing that they're perfectly safe. Usually by the second climb, however, they're ready to go farther, and they almost always want to know how high they went. Teens generally head straight to the top and ask for more. In fact, after your first climb, staff will adjust the difficulty of climbs two and three based on how everyone feels. Chances are, by the end, you'll feel good *and* tired.

HEY, KIDS! There's no one right way to climb. Pick the rocks that feel comfortable for you, remembering that you can put both hands on one rock or reach around a corner. The staff might make a suggestion, like "put your left hand on that green rock" or "just straighten your legs," but you're free to make your own way. Remember, also, that this is a noncompetitive sport. You don't have to measure your success against how high a sibling or parent goes. Measure it by how much fun you have.

GROUNDS FOR SCULPTURE

Stroll around the grounds until you feel at home. It won't take long at this sculpture garden founded by J. Seward Johnson, Jr., in 1992. Unlike indoor museums, which some children find inhibiting, the Grounds for Sculpture is liberating. Kids can peek, pose and ponder, draw, and romp (respectfully) around these 22 acres densely dotted with 150 artworks. Though the sculptures here are all contemporary, they are quite varied. Both abstract and representational, they include all sorts of subjects and media. Works in metal, stone, wood, cement, and fiberglass range from the somber (*Depression Bread Line*) to the whimsical (the shiny red *Summertime Lady*). Johnson's own statues look plucked from the 19th century; in fact, some are re-creations of famous Impressionist paintings.

Ways to approach the sculpture are equally varied. Ask your kids what a piece "is" before reading its title. From the back, for example, *Sacred Grove* looks more like a hen with chicks than trees. Pick up "Sculpture Search in the Park," which encourages kids to hunt for artworks with certain shapes, themes, materials, or finishes. Those disinclined to this

EATS FOR KIDS Dining amid the trees and sculptures (one even joins you for lunch) is a wonderful experience. Unfortunately you can't picnic here, and the **Café** (tel. 609/890–6015), open 10–4, exhibits uneven execution of its interesting menu (from pastrami and portobello sandwiches to chicken nuggets). The **Gazebo** sells beverages and light snacks May–October. Despite being named for a *Wind in the Willows* character, **Rat's** (tel. 609/584–7800), also on the grounds, is an expensive restaurant better reserved for teens. Casual options include **Kramer's Bagels** (1700 Nottingham Way, tel. 609/586–3113) and **Peking House** (1664 Nottingham Way, tel. 609/586–6111).

18 Fairgrounds Rd., Hamilton, NJ

 609/586-0616

 T-Th, $4 ages 13 and up, $3 students; F-Sa, $7 ages 13 and up, $6 students, $3 children 12 and under; Su, $10

T-Su 10-9

6 and up

art-appreciation lesson can opt for their own studio class. Most children love to capture their favorite works on paper or film (bring sketch pads and cameras), posing with the sculptures and having you pose, too.

The landscape here invites as much exploration as the sculptures. Trees, fountains, hedges, ponds, and bamboo stands create changing prospects. Turn a corner, and you'll discover another statue and landscape. Open a door in a hedge to enter Wonderland, but instead of a bottle that says "drink me," you'll find a woman with a gold-lined head or other sculpture. Most works outdoors are permanent or on loan for several years at a time, but two buildings display changing exhibits. Be sure to visit the impressive Water Garden, adjacent to the Domestic Arts building—yet another unusual setting in which to view these very unusual works of art.

GETTING THERE Take I-95 north to I-295 south (I-295 north from southern New Jersey) to Exit 65B/Sloane Avenue west. Then stay to the right, and follow signs for the Grounds for Sculpture. Artworks placed along the way provide a preview of what's to come.

KEEP IN MIND Though the grounds offer kids freedom, it only goes so far. Kids shouldn't touch or climb on statues—for the art's and your children's safety—or bother the resident peacocks. Keep an eye peeled at all times, as it's easy to lose track of busy youngsters. As for subject matter, be warned that some sculptures might spark questions. Among the many human forms, some are nude or semi-nude. Other pieces, such as the self-explanatory *Skewered* and *Acheron*, a boat of bones floating near the Gazebo, might raise different issues. Yet somehow, nothing seems too unsettling in this serene, pastoral setting.

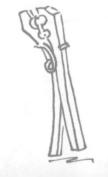

HAGLEY MUSEUM

41

Delaware is DuPont country, and the site of the Hagley Museum—not a standard museum at all, but rather an outdoor industrial-history interpretive center—was its first company town. On 230 acres along the picturesque Brandywine River, your family can learn about the early days of an empire and, more interesting for kids, about the making of gunpowder.

Start in the Henry Clay Mill, the visitor center, for a brief orientation film and a trip through the exhibit room. Button pushers will be happy here, as many dioramas include moving parts, illustrating mill processes and telling du Pont history. Admission includes a bus ride to the du Pont family home, Eleutherian Mills, but frankly, family furnishings and a formal French garden don't have the kid appeal of the abandoned 19th-century mill and the adjacent Blacksmith Hill community.

Walking or taking the bus to the mill yields a deceptively peaceful but beautiful view of stone buildings nestled between the millrace and the river. With potential explosions

GETTING THERE Take I–95 south to Exit 8B in Delaware. Follow U.S. 202 north for 1 3/10 miles. Turn left onto Route 141. After 2 miles, turn right onto the Tyler-McConnell Bridge and watch for the Hagley entrance, on the right.

EATS FOR KIDS On Blacksmith Hill, **Just Desserts Café** (Belin House, tel. 302/622–9030) doesn't just serve desserts but also soups, sandwiches, and salads. A picnic area is on site, too. In nearby Greenville, the family-oriented **Brandywine Brewing Company and Restaurant** (3801 Kennett Pike, tel. 302/655–8000) has sandwiches, burgers, salads, and kid food. The brew at **BrewHaHa** (Kennett Pike, Powder Mill Sq., Greenville, tel. 302/658–6336) is of a different type: coffee. The coffee shop is open breakfast, lunch, and dinner and serves up sandwiches, salads, and pastries. Also see the Delaware Museum of Natural History.

 Rte. 141, Wilmington, DE

 302/658-2400

 $9.75 ages 15 and up, $7.50 students, $3.50 children 6–14

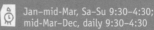 Jan–mid-Mar, Sa–Su 9:30–4:30; mid-Mar–Dec, daily 9:30–4:30

 5 and up

in mind, the mills were built as small thick-walled buildings, standing at arm's length to one another with one side open to the water; that way, any explosions would be contained and directed river-ward. A display on the black-powder-making process, in the Millright Shop, is adjacent to the old belt-driven Machine Shop, where demonstrations are held. Demonstrations at the Roll Mill pack a bigger punch, however. A sluice gate is opened, and water pours into the sump, powering 1,600-pound rolling wheels. For the grand finale, some black powder is tested, producing quite a bang.

Walk up the hill and through the gates to Blacksmith Hill. Though the blacksmith shop isn't open, you can tour the restored Gibbons House (the foreman's home) and talk to costumed interpreters. Kids like practicing penmanship with a quill pen in the one-room Sunday school, where once a week mill workers' children were taught to read and write before the advent of public education. It's just another reminder of how different things were a long time ago.

HEY, KIDS! The mill was a dangerous place: 288 accidental explosions claimed 228 lives in its 119-year history. To keep sparks from igniting the powder, no metal was allowed in the mill area. That meant no belt buckles or metal shovels (wooden ones were used for the powder). Even lunch pails had to be left outside the gate. Incidentally, explosions weren't the only danger here. Machines in the machine shop took their toll, too. According to a former machinist, you could tell how long someone had worked in the shop by how many fingertips he was missing. Yuck.

HEDGEROW THEATRE FOR CHILDREN

A rustic 1840s stone gristmill by a little stream under the trees—it's just the kind of setting you'd expect for a fairy tale. You could easily imagine seeing seven dwarfs whistling away up the stream or Rapunzel combing her golden hair by the window. The truth is, there are *real* fairy tales going on here, but they take place on stage, with an audience full of shouting, giggling, and singing kids watching.

Once upon a time many years ago, the Hedgerow Theatre began mounting weekly children's performances in addition to its regular main-stage productions. Every Saturday at 11 (and very occasionally at 1), you can sit on the cushioned benches in the 144-seat theater and watch tried-and-true kids' plays, such as *Cinderella, The Wind in the Willows,* and *Beauty and the Beast.* Performances last for under an hour, and shows run for five to ten weeks. To add to the fun, they're often full of audience participation.

Don't expect cutting-edge drama here. These are simple productions with simple sets and

EATS FOR KIDS **Pinocchio's Restaurant** (131 E. Baltimore Pike, tel. 610/566–7767) dishes up pizza, stromboli, and pasta and gives kids dough to play with while they're waiting. Every once in a while, the actors go here after a show. If you're not in the Italian-eat mood, you can opt for dependable ol' **Friendly's** (1145 W. Baltimore Pike, tel. 610/891–0188). If you'd rather bring lunch, you can take advantage of the theater's lovely setting and eat at one of the picnic tables by the stream in back.

64 Rose Valley Rd., Media

 $6

 Sa 11

 610/565-4211

 3-11

musical accompaniments. Casts usually consist of adult actors from Hedgerow's resident theater company but may also have child actors, including those who are part of the Hedgerow Theatre School. As a result, talent can vary. Parents might happen upon a performance that doesn't quite have the quality they were expecting, but one look around the audience at the smiling, engaged children, and you'll realize that polish isn't always everything.

After performances, juice and cookies are put out, and the actors mill around in the beam-ceilinged lobby to talk to interested theatergoers.

For all its artistic offerings, Philadelphia doesn't have a lot of regularly scheduled children's theater. It's nice to know that on any given Saturday, you can go to the Hedgerow for a dependable family favorite that'll put your children in that happily ever after mood—at least for the afternoon.

KEEP IN MIND
Other area theater companies present outstanding professional performances for children—with many new plays or new adaptations—but their schedules are more intermittent. See the Arden Children's Theatre and the Mum Puppettheatre, both in Philadelphia, and the People's Light & Theatre Company, in Malvern.

GETTING THERE Take I-95 south past the airport to I-476 north (the Blue Route). Get off at Exit 2, and turn left on Baltimore Pike (direction: Media). After about 1½ miles, turn left onto Manchester Avenue; Dunkin' Donuts is on the corner. After you pass the Rose Valley train station, Manchester turns into Rose Valley Road. When you see the yellow flashing light above the road, look for the old stone theater on your left.

HERR'S SNACK FACTORY TOUR

Does your family like watching machines and conveyor belts repetitively crank out familiar products before your very eyes? And do you like pretzels, corn and tortilla chips, popcorn, cheese curls, or potato chips? If so, follow your nose on this classic factory tour, which takes you past various stages in the making of Herr's products. Just as it's hard to stop eating after only a few chips, so, too, is it hard to stop watching all the contraptions that mix, cut, extrude, puff, bake, fry, season, quality-check, package, and move the huge amounts of snack food around this large plant.

Upon arrival at the Visitor Center, you'll be assigned to a tour—perhaps "Ketchup," "Salt & Vinegar," or "Smokey BBQ"—named for Herr's potato chip flavors (16 and counting). Tours start with a somewhat cutesy video about Herr's history, "The Tastiest Tour in Town." It, like the video snippets at each stop, stars Chipper, Herr's chipmunk mascot, and his annoying (at least to many adults) robot friend, CC. Luckily, tour

KEEP IN MIND Though Herr's is about 1½ hours from Center City on U.S. 1, it's worth the trip, especially if combined with another attraction (see Brandywine River Museum and Longwood Gardens). Confirm the best route when you call for reservations, which are recommended, especially during school breaks.

EATS FOR KIDS You can get hot dogs, chicken nuggets, PB&Js, and the like at **Chipper's Cafe,** an inexpensive snack bar in the Herr's Visitor Center. Plenty of tables are available, and you can even reserve ahead to have your child's birthday here. (You supply the cake; Herr's provides a Chipper doll.) For table service amid automobile-theme decor, plus homemade soups, burgers, sandwiches, and more Herr's potato chips, head across the street to **Nottingham Breakfast House** (Rte. 272, tel. 610/ 932–0825), formerly Johnny's Burgers. Or ask at the Visitor Center for suggestions of family restaurants at other exits along U.S. 1.

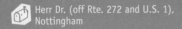

guides appeal to kids and grown-ups alike as they explain how each product is made—and how anything that doesn't pass muster is sent to Mr. Herr's snack-loving cows. Since each process is surprisingly different, even small children remain interested for the hour or so the tour takes, and a taste of fresh potato chips right off the line holds grumbling stomachs in check.

It's hard not to be impressed by the numbers: 4,000 pounds of pretzels, 1,000 pounds of cheese curls and popcorn, and 10,000 pounds of potato chips produced *per hour*. Anyone bored on the drive home can do a little math to really drive home the scope of what they saw: *If 8 to 10 tractor-trailers of potatoes (50,000 pounds each) are used each day, and it takes 4 pounds of potatoes to make 1 pound of chips, how many pounds of chips are made daily?* If your kids prefer scientific research to math, simply open a few bags and let everyone decide which flavor they like best.

HEY, KIDS! Guess what Herr's onion rings are made of. (Warning: This is a trick question.) The answer is potatoes. Little orange-color rings of dehydrated potato flakes are puffed up to look like real onion rings and are flavored with onion seasoning so they taste like onion rings. Don't worry: They taste better than they sound. So if your tour guide asks the question, you'll be ready to impress him or her—not to mention your parents, as long as they don't read this—with your noshing knowledge. To every other question, answer "to the cows." Trust us on this.

HOWELL LIVING HISTORY FARM

38

Ask today's kids where flour comes from, and many will answer, "the supermarket." That can be remedied at Howell Farm, a re-created 1900-era family farm that, true to the ideals of living history, lets children learn about both farming and history in a way that's meaningful to them—by getting involved and asking questions.

Leave the 21st century in the parking lot and walk past snake fences, planted fields, and pastureland to a white farmhouse and red outbuildings, including a barn, chicken coop, and corncrib. You can take a self-guided tour anytime the farm is open, perhaps wading in the creek or watching the farmer plowing behind a team of horses. Come on a Saturday, however, and your kids can really take part. Every week brings a different program—from milking a cow to tapping a sugar maple to shearing sheep. Over a year, you could help harvest ice, wheat, honey, potatoes, or popcorn. Each program also has a small associated craft project.

EATS FOR KIDS   To preserve historic authenticity, picnics are restricted to tables near the parking lot. The visitor center will sell some food, while the farmhouse sells a more historically accurate Saturday lunch. Head south 4 miles to the drive-in-like **Fifty's** (Rte. 29, tel. 609/737–0505), open early March–late October, for fried chicken, flavored sodas, egg creams, and *big* ice cream cones (double and triple scoops, though available, seem physically impossible). Two miles north, breakfast or lunch at Lambertville's **Full Moon** (23 Bridge St., tel. 609/397–1096) includes interesting twists (e.g., sun-dried tomatoes, goat cheese) on burgers, eggs, salads, and sandwiches.

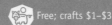

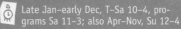
Other seasonal, but not necessarily historically appropriate, farm fun is held at the farm's modern facilities at Belle Mountain, near Route 29. For several years, fall has brought the Amazing Maize Maze, where you could not only navigate a corn maze but also pick up "kernels of knowledge." Answering questions and collecting puzzle pieces would reveal a map to help you out. Other activities here might include horse-drawn tours of local hills and dales and a pizza farm, a circular tract where each "slice" is devoted to a pizza ingredient (tomatoes, wheat for the crust, herbs and spices, and so on), culminating in—you guessed it—making a pizza. Call ahead to find out if and when one of these activities is happening, and to check fees. But whatever does go on here, it, like the rest of the farm, will be designed as much for ag-education as it is for agri-tainment. Just maybe, today's kids will learn about where their food comes from and how families lived a century ago.

GETTING THERE Take I–95 north. When you cross the river into New Jersey, exit onto Route 29 north. After 7 miles, at Valley Road, you'll see the sign for the farm. Turn right, and follow the road for 1½ miles to Howell Farm, on your left.

KEEP IN MIND To keep the farm historic, most modern items, including a new visitor center being built near the parking lot, are kept off-site. Please restrict modern equipment, like Frisbees, to this area, too. For recreation in the farm area, try rolling a hoop, or come on a day when old-time baseball is being played. Though cell phones are not banned, consider how silly it would be if your phone rang during a plowing match. And yes, in addition to vintage fun, there are vintage gifts to buy, including horseshoes ($2) onto which the blacksmith will punch your child's initials.

INDEPENDENCE NATIONAL
HISTORICAL PARK

Picture Philadelphia's most historic landmarks, and chances are you'll also picture tourists and class trips. But local families, too, can and should explore this wonderful national park woven into the fabric of Old City. A visit can be accomplished in small doses or a full day.

Start at the appropriate visitor center, where you can watch the film *Independence* and pick up a map and schedule. Some programs are designed for children (few on winter weekdays, but plentiful daily in summer), many of them at Franklin Court (*see above*). Take your pick of sights, but don't miss Independence Hall and the Liberty Bell.

To see Independence Hall, called the State House in the Founding Fathers' time, you'll need to take the short tour. Line up behind the building (on summer days, late afternoon is generally less busy), and proceed into the East Wing for a brief orientation by a ranger. Then it's into the main building to see the courtroom and Assembly Room, where the

HEY, KIDS!
Want to join the Continental Army? If you have what it takes, including two front teeth, enlist with Gen. Washington during his Call to Arms on summer afternoons. It's part of Historic Philadelphia, Inc.'s Town Crier Summer Theatre (*see below*).

KEEP IN MIND
The park is undergoing its first big changes since the Bicentennial. Slated to open in late 2001, the Independence Visitor Center will be information central for both the park and the region. By spring 2002, the Liberty Bell should be in its new pavilion at 6th and Chestnut, with additional exhibit space. (The old pavilion—"with the charm and warmth of a drive-up bank," as one park staffer described it—was designed so it wouldn't be mistaken for a historic structure.) Also planned for the new Independence Mall (spring 2003), the modern, interactive National Constitution Center will explore that document and its impact.

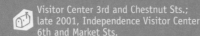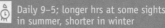

Visitor Center 3rd and Chestnut Sts.; late 2001, Independence Visitor Center 6th and Market Sts.

215/597-8974

Free; Portrait Gallery $2 ages 17 and up; house tours $2 ages 17 and up

Daily 9–5; longer hrs at some sights in summer, shorter in winter

5 and up

Declaration of Independence, Articles of Confederation, and Constitution first breathed life. Except for Washington's "rising sun" chair—so called because, after the Constitution was adopted, Franklin happily declared that the half sun on its back represented "a rising and not a setting sun"—furnishings aren't original, but it hardly detracts from the feeling that history was made here. You can also visit upstairs, with nice furnishings but not the same history. The West Wing's Great Essentials exhibit includes the park's copies of the Declaration, Articles of Confederation, and Constitution (a proof copy with typo, marked by George Washington) and the silver inkstand used in signing.

To visit the Liberty Bell, cross Chestnut Street. During open hours, rangers give brief talks about the origins of the bell, the folklore behind its crack, and how what was once simply the State House Bell became a symbol of independence worldwide. But then the whole park is full of the history and symbolism of what this country was meant to be.

EATS FOR KIDS   John Adams once praised the original **City Tavern** (*see* Lights of Liberty) as "the most genteel" tavern in America. Today a reconstruction stands on the site and is actually part of the park. Franklin's name rather than his actual presence graces **Benny's Place** (435 Chestnut St., tel. 215/574–FOOD), a casual spot whose menu has everything from soup to chocolate nut sundaes, plus breakfast. *Also see* other Old City sights for more suggestions.

INDEPENDENCE SEAPORT MUSEUM

You'll find watercraft, watercraft everywhere at this maritime museum 90 miles upriver from the ocean. Exhibits detail local history—of Philadelphia's port and of the Delaware River, Bay, and tributaries—and a submarine and early 20th-century warship open for exploration expand the focus further.

Walk up the Delaware Bay and River (watch the carpet) and under the Ben Franklin Bridge to the museum's main exhibit: Home Port Philadelphia. Those patient enough to look at models and read descriptions will learn about immigration, the navy, shipbuilding, and merchant shipping. Those more inclined to romp than read can climb in a "floating" rowboat or in a cramped steerage berth. (The back seat of the car doesn't look so bad, now does it?) Kids can use a crane to move shipping containers from barge to train and back, or drop a line, hopefully for fish, not trash. Though most displays aren't interactive, there are enough to keep little hands busy for a while. Older kids and adults might be interested in the boat-building facility, where classes are offered.

HEY, KIDS! Have fun on the *Olympia* by looking for items and figuring out their puzzles. For example, why did the barbershop double as a dental clinic? (What did they have in common?) Why does "scuttlebutt," the name for a ship's drinking fountain, also mean gossip? (Picture the water cooler at your parents' work.) Why did Admiral Dewey wear his Battle of Manila Bay medal backward? (Whose face is on the medal, and how boastful would that be?) And why is he remembered for the unmemorable quote, "You may fire when ready, Gridley"? (There may not be an answer for that one.)

Penn's Landing at 211
S. Columbus Blvd. and Walnut St.

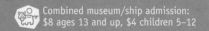 Combined museum/ship admission:
$8 ages 13 and up, $4 children 5–12

 Daily 10–5

215/925–5439

 6 and up

Outside and downriver, walk from stem to stern in the U.S.S. *Becuna,* a World War II– to Vietnam War–era sub with the smell of age. In the forward torpedo room, notice how close to the torpedoes the men slept. Though no berths are spacious, higher-ranking sleepers got a little more room. You'll travel through the control room, filled with buttons and switches; past the radio room, complete with Betty Grable pin-up; and beyond the main galley, mess, and engine rooms to the aft torpedo room, before coming up for air.

The *Becuna'*s big older neighbor, the U.S.S. *Olympia,* was a symbol of the modern American navy at the turn of the last century. Clamber around her two lower decks and topsides to get a picture of life aboard this warship—minus the gunfire. In fact, during your museum visit, you'll voyage from the Delaware River to Manila Bay, cruising through 100 years in a few hours.

EATS FOR KIDS
Eventually there will be restaurants in the new Penn's Landing entertainment complex. In the meantime, head to **Spasso** (34 S. Front St., tel. 215/ 592–7661) for good Italian food, or to a number of other nearby restaurants (*see* Go Vertical or any Old City listing).

KEEP IN MIND Two pass options provide discounts if you're planning on visiting other Philly attractions along with the museum and its ships. RiverPass, for example, also includes a round-trip on the Penn's Landing RiverLink Ferry (right outside the museum), as well as admission to the New Jersey State Aquarium & Camden Children's Garden. CityPass covers the seaport museum and ships, the aquarium and children's garden, the Philadelphia Art Museum, Franklin Institute, Philadelphia Zoo, and Academy of Natural Sciences. See separate listings for these attractions.

JOHN HEINZ NATIONAL WILDLIFE REFUGE AT TINICUM

Pennsylvania is known for hills and mountains, woods and farmland. It's not generally known for tidal wetlands, but that's what you'll find—along with the profusion of wildlife the ecosystem attracts—at this refuge right in southeastern Philadelphia.

The new Cusano Environmental Education Center can furnish you with a map and brochures on the wildlife you just might encounter at the refuge. Over 280 species of birds have been spotted here, which isn't at all surprising since the area is on the Atlantic Flyway and is a popular rest stop during spring and fall migrations. You'll see some birds, perhaps skimming along the water to feast on insects, and hear more. Frogs, turtles, and butterflies are here, too, as are deer, muskrats, and mice.

You can choose to follow the Dike Trail, between Darby Creek and the Impoundment (a large pond covered in spatterdock plants), or take the Haul Road, which leads from the environmental center around the other side of the Impoundment. From this road, you

GETTING THERE

Take I–95 toward the airport, and exit on Route 291 (Lester). Turn right at the first light (Bartram Avenue), left at the second light (84th Street), and left at the second light again (Lindbergh Boulevard). Buses 37 and 108 also serve the refuge.

EATS FOR KIDS

The refuge is close to the airport, and you'll find a number of choices in airport hotels and the airport itself. Embassy Suites has the **Embassy Grill** (9000 Bartram Ave., tel. 215/365–4500 ext. 1042), which does have a kids' menu. The airport has a **T.G.I. Friday's** (B–C connector, tel. 215/365–4300), near the food court between the B and C concourses. The bad news for parents is you'll have to pay to park; the good news for little kids is you can stay and watch the planes. For more local options, see the listing for Fort Mifflin.

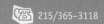

can walk out on a boardwalk over the Impoundment and soak up quite a view. (Repair of the hurricane-ravaged section that connects to the Dike Trail is planned.)

About ¾ mile down the Dike Trail is the first observation area, a two-story tower from which you can see across the Impoundment toward the airport. A second observation point, a bird blind, is about another ½ mile farther on the Darby Creek side, by now widened into a tidal marsh. In all, the refuge has 10 miles of trails and half a dozen observation areas.

If you're not content to simply walk and watch, bring a rod and reel for some catch-and-release fishing, a canoe (launch available), bicycle, or camera. Thanks to the new environmental center, family nature programs combining talks and walks are now offered year-round. The center also adds an indoor viewing area with scopes and exhibit space—on the refuge's natural and cultural history, endangered species, and conservation education—to what was already a vast outdoor display of wetland ecology.

KEEP IN MIND Though the Dike Trail is flat, it's largely un-sheltered from the sun, so bring water bottles and sunscreen. Haul Road is a lot shadier. Mosquitoes aren't as bad a problem as you might think, but always check for ticks, even though the trails are wide and gravel covered. Speaking of gravel, pushing small-wheeled strollers is tough going, but don't let that keep you from bringing little ones (backpacks help). Diaper graduates should use the facilities at the environmental education center; after that there's just one port-o-pot by the first observation area.

LIGHTS OF LIBERTY

"Enjoy your revolution!" bids the person who hands you your headset. It's hard not to, from the moment a pair of patriots in scarlet waistcoats open the door for you at PECO's Liberty Center until the Declaration of Independence is signed, sealed, and delivered at Independence Hall. "Your revolution" is, in fact, a one-hour sound-and-light show–cum–nighttime walking tour around some of the historic district's famous sights.

Children and adults are given headsets with different narrations: kids' version by Whoopi Goldberg, adults' by Ossie Davis, with help from Walter Cronkite, Charlton Heston, Claire Bloom, and others. Whoopi's narration is a little simpler and more fun—especially when she calls George III a brat. From the Liberty Center you follow your guides to Franklin Court, Carpenters' Hall, the Second Bank of the United States, a smoky battlefield (watch for a surprise here), and finally Independence Hall. (To learn more, visit these sights when they're open during the day; *see* Independence National Historical Park and Franklin Court.) At each stop, another act in the revolutionary drama unfolds, augmented by multistory im-

EATS FOR KIDS   Next door to the Liberty Center is casual **Willie & Duffy's** (*see* Ghost Tour of Philadelphia). To really go Colonial, dine at **City Tavern** (138 S. 2nd St., tel. 215/413–1443). Yes, it's frequented by tourists, and yes, you can get cheaper food elsewhere, but how many Philadelphia restaurants offer a kids' menu of turkey pot pie, prime rib, cornmeal-encrusted chicken fingers, and, as a drink, shrub (fruit vinegar mixed with sugar and Sprite), served by waiters in Colonial garb? The building, a reconstruction of the original City Tavern (circa 1773), is owned by the National Park Service. Also see other Old City sights.

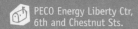 PECO Energy Liberty Ctr,
6th and Chestnut Sts.

 215/LIBERTY or
877/GO-2-1776

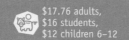 $17.76 adults,
$16 students,
$12 children 6–12

 Apr–late May and early Sept–Oct, Th–Sa;
Memorial Day–Labor Day, T–Sa; tours every
15 min starting at sunset

 6 and up

ages projected onto buildings, smoke (but no mirrors), and a "3-D" surround-sound system that makes you want to step out of the way when you hear hoofbeats behind you. Amazingly, the equipment is set up and dismantled every night.

The history that's told delves more deeply into this familiar territory than you probably remember from junior high. You see not only Colonists' anger over the Stamp Tax but also their ambivalence and discord over independence before making the decision to secede. In addition to hearing from well-known white patriot men like Thomas Paine and John Adams, you hear about women and Loyalists from the words of Deborah and William Franklin, Ben's wife and son. An effort is also made to fill in gaps concerning African-Americans. In fact, the adult-version narrator, James Forten, is a black naval hero taken prisoner by the British. Your revolution won't be the cheapest hour you'll ever spend, but there isn't another one quite like it around.

HEY, KIDS! Don't be shy about calling out "Fie!" or "Down with the British!" or singing along with "God Bless America" at the end of the show. Remember: Since you and everyone else will be wearing headsets, no one will hear you.

KEEP IN MIND You can reserve tickets over the phone; to reschedule, just call back. The show runs in light drizzle (ponchos and umbrellas available) but not in significant rain. Arrive at the stars-and-stripes-draped center ½ hour early to pick up the appropriate headset and mind-set. Costumed actors mill about, chatting and leading your merry band of 40 or 50 revolutionaries in a bawdy song. The show is fun for elementary schoolkids but best for those who've learned some of the history, and though the kids' channel is recommended for ages 6–12, it's not cutesy and can be enjoyed by teens and adults, too.

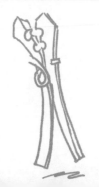

LONGWOOD GARDENS

I t's huge, it's constantly changing, and when it calls itself a "horticultural showplace," it's not lying. Longwood Gardens is an enormous attraction. Covering 1,050 outdoor acres and a gigantic conservatory, it has 20 outdoor and 20 indoor gardens including 11,000 types of plants—assuming anyone could ever count them. Over the course of a year, the gardens transition through eight festival seasons, meaning that you can come back repeatedly and always see something different.

Spring starts early here (January, to be exact) with indoor flowering bulbs. By summer, there are roses, water lilies, and outdoor sound-and-light fountain displays. Autumn brings vibrant fall foliage and a chrysanthemum festival, and Christmas is known for exuberant holiday finery, including designer trees, poinsettias, carolers, organ sing-alongs, and whimsical topiary. Displays in the Conservatory range from diminutive bonsai, some of which have been trained for over 50 years, to towering palms—some positively prehistoric-looking—in the lush Palm House.

HEY, KIDS!
To describe everything at the gardens that's done especially for kids is impossible. Pick up a copy of the Kids Map or check it out ahead of time in the Fun for Kids section at www.longwoodgardens.org, and choose where you want to go.

KEEP IN MIND
That which makes the gardens so impressive—size—is also what can make them overwhelming and/or boring for youngsters. Tour buses disgorge their contents regularly, and the walking required, especially if mom and dad want to see "one more garden," can be tiring. Don't bite off more than little ones can chew, but don't worry, either; no matter what you see, there will always be more the next visit. In December, planning becomes even more essential, since almost everything is inside. Come early in the season, on weekdays, and during the day to avoid the hordes crammed into the Conservatory.

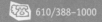 U.S. 1, Kennett Square

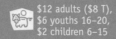 $12 adults ($8 T),
$6 youths 16–20,
$2 children 6–15

 Jan–Mar and Nov, daily 9–5; Apr–Oct, daily 9–6,
with longer hrs T, Th, Sat June–Aug; late Nov–Dec 9–9;
conservatory opens at 10

 610/388–1000

All ages

But aside from all the pretty and exotic flowers, which may or may not interest your children as much as they do you, Longwood Gardens has a host of spaces created specifically for kids. The Children's Garden in the Conservatory is a pint-size maze of hedges, fountains, a ruin, and trees. Some parents try to follow their children under the low archways and through crawlable tunnels; veterans wait near an entrance.

Outside, kids' gardens proliferate, too. Children might become enchanted by an edible alphabetical garden, a maize maze of Indian corn, a tree hunt, or a lake where feeding the fish is definitely encouraged (and appreciated by the fish). A waterfall and fountains, concerts and theatrical performances, topiary, and a Kids Corner activity center are some more, but not all, of the attractions here for junior horticulturists. On the way out, if you spy your child's thumb starting to turn green, stop by the Longwood Gardens Shop. Here, in addition to traditional gifty things, you can buy plants to start your own very miniature Longwood at home.

EATS FOR KIDS The **Terrace Restaurant** (tel. 610/388–6771) building has two dining choices: a full-service restaurant with tablecloths (but also a kids' menu), open March–December, and a less-expensive and kid-eas-ier cafeteria. Watch for the cafeteria's value meals, for both adults and kids, which ring in at $2.95 for kids 10 and under. Daring young eaters can try some-thing made with the local specialty—mushrooms. A picnic area, adjacent to the gardens on Longwood Road, is open April–October.

MERCER MUSEUM

Walk up concrete stairs that echo with unknown footsteps; past a vampire-killing kit with silver bullets, a wooden stake, and powdered garlic; and into a tall chamber where old vehicles and implements dangle overhead. No, you haven't entered the Twilight Zone, or even a bad dream; you've just discovered the Mercer Museum.

Another creation of archaeologist/architect/artisan Henry Mercer (*see* Fonthill), this funky seven-story concrete museum contains a huge collection of everyday, pre-industrial objects displayed in decidedly un-everyday ways. From 1895 to 1915, Mercer collected these artifacts—considered junk by many at the time—in order to document a rapidly disappearing way of life. The unusual displays were intended not just to fit a lot (50,000 objects) into the available space but also to get people to look at these ordinary objects in extraordinary ways. The most striking view is from the Central Court, looking up at many levels oozing with such articles as a Conestoga wagon, whaling ship, and fire engine. To see these big items from other angles, climb the small staircases to the upper floors. Lining the museum's

EATS FOR KIDS   To continue the 19th-century theme, stop by **Roosevelt's Blue Star Restaurant** (52 E. State St., tel. 215/348–9000)—Theodore Roosevelt, that is. The menu ranges from Teddy's club sandwich to Chilean sea bass, and though there's no separate menu for kids, they'll like the homemade potato chips, pizza, and burgers (buffalo, ostrich, or beef). Order good, quick meals—sandwiches, burgers, and cheese steaks—at the counter of **Hoagie Works** (44 E. State St., tel. 215/348–7066), and sit at Formica tables with vinyl chairs. Just try leaving without succumbing to the bakery in front.

84 S. Pine St., Doylestown

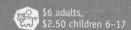 $6 adults,
$2.50 children 6–17

 M and W–Sa 10–5, T 10–9, Su 12–5

 215/345–0210

4 and up

perimeter are rooms crammed with items, especially tools, organized by Early American trade or such categories as fruit preservation and lighting devices. While perusing all this stuff, your children might even learn a thing or two—like what a cooper makes or that tanning isn't just done at the beach.

Kids are drawn to the odd and ghoulish: the aforementioned vampire kit, a hearse and nearby gallows (which you stand underneath), real tortoiseshell hair combs adjacent to a preserved tortoiseshell (yes, there was life before plastic), and such old-fashioned remedies as Foley's Honey and Tar Compound (yum!) in a country store brimming with goods. Also keep your eyes peeled for a handful of stations where kids can *do* something: make crayon rubbings of tiles (lobby), drive a simulated buggy, don Early American clothes, weave felt strips, or build a log house. In fact, most children love these simple, nonmotorized, hands-on activities. Henry Mercer would be proud.

GETTING THERE Take either Route 611 or U.S. 202 into Doylestown, and look for signs to the Doylestown Cultural District. A block off Main Street and two blocks off State Street, the museum is across from the Michener Art Museum. But if you're that close, you're there.

HEY, KIDS! With all the treasures here, it's sometimes hard to focus on individual items. To help you, pick up an audio guide (there's a fun kids' channel) and look for the yellow-labeled objects; grab a worksheet on your way up the stairs; or go treasure hunting for things that start with each letter of the alphabet. For example, can you find an animal horn, bathtub, cigar store figures, dog pawprints, and other items all the way to zithers? We promise that it's possible. If you really look at objects, instead of running from room to room, it's amazing what you'll find.

MORRIS ARBORETUM

Victorian garden: The very words are enough to send a chill through any family with energetic children in search of something to *do*, rather than see. Chill not! The Morris Arboretum is a warm and welcoming place—graceful yet fanciful, strollable yet rompable. It's a wonderful outing for families of all ages, from youngsters to their grandparents.

The plantings are gorgeous, of course. A formal rose garden with fountain is so lovely that even kids appreciate it, wondering, as one child did, "Why can't we have this at home?" (Start weeding now.) But the arboretum's real draws for children are its unusual finds and decidedly un-prissy air. As testament to the latter, for example, you might see fairy rings, circles of mushrooms growing up, unmowed, in the lawn. Beds with neatly aligned annuals are the exception, rather than the norm, here.

As for unusual finds, a log cabin beside a babbling brook has a functioning pump outside and a stone fireplace inside. Discover the secret passageway under the Mercury Temple

HEY, KIDS!
Try to recognize the landmarks in the Garden Railway—many of them representing places mentioned in this book: Independence Hall, the Betsy Ross House, Elfreth's Alley, the Japanese House in Fairmount Park, Boathouse Row boathouses, Washington's Headquarters at Valley Forge, and even the arboretum's Fernery.

KEEP IN MIND Arb etiquette is as follows: You are invited to leave the winding paths at any time, run on the grass, and touch—but don't pick—the plants. You can scamper around the sculptures, but please don't climb on them or the trees. Though it's not officially sanctioned, kids invariably end up wading in the garden fountains, including the Step Fountain, where water shoots out of three lions' mouths and cascades down a rippling stairway. Parents of children who have sensitive skin or who still put hands to mouth should know that the water is treated to prevent algae growth.

100 Northwestern Ave.
(off Germantown Ave.)

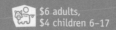
$6 adults,
$4 children 6–17

215/247-5777

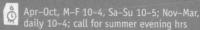
Apr–Oct, M–F 10–4, Sa–Su 10–5; Nov–Mar,
daily 10–4; call for summer evening hrs

All ages

into a secret grotto that leads into the Ravine Garden. The Swan Pond has everyone's favorite, though territorial (keep your distance), floating white birds, while in the Sculpture Garden, an enormous bronze bullfrog with a bemused expression peers out from a stand of bamboo. Perhaps the most unusual display is the Fernery, a century-old, glass-roofed building lush with ferns. Circle the warm room, past vegetation growing from every face, through a rock tunnel, and over a bridge above a waterfall-spilled pond of goldfish, all named Bob.

As with all gardens, you'll be tempted to come after Mother's Day, but it's better to wait until Father's Day, when the Garden Railway reappears. Model trains from a trolley to an Amtrak run through a beautiful tree-shaded landscape. Trestles made of sticks take trains over your head, into the trees, and past models of famous buildings made of bark, twigs, and moss. If your kids ask to have something like this at home, you'll have to do a lot more than weeding.

EATS FOR KIDS Open for lunch daily and those summer evenings when the arboretum is open, the **Solaris Café** sells sandwiches, burgers, and salads that can be eaten at tables behind the visitor center. You may eat your own picnic here, too. **Bruno's** (9800 Germantown Ave., tel. 215/242–1880) is a local favorite for sandwiches, Philly steaks, pastas, hoagies, burgers (you can ask for a child-size burger), and milk shakes as well as breakfast. Eat outside on screened or unscreened porches or inside at the counter or in a red vinyl booth near, what else?, a jukebox.

MUM PUPPETTHEATRE

A hand, a Styrofoam ball, a telephone, a miniature baseball bat, and not one word: That's all Mum Puppettheatre needs to turn an audience full of 3- to 10-year-olds and their parents into a bunch of laughing hyenas.

Mum's approach to theater is different from that of regular human-actor-based companies, not to mention old-fashioned puppet shows à la Punch and Judy—so much so that it sometimes takes parents a moment to adjust. No, Mum has nothing to do with the Mummers, and it isn't some British bloke's mother. Rather it refers to the completely wordless (though not soundless, as music is often used) nature of almost all performances. Children have little trouble with this concept, as they are generally more comfortable than their parents at creating an explanation for what's happening and then moving on.

The puppets used can be traditional hand or stick puppets, rarely marionettes, but more often something unusual and created from scratch. According to Robert Smythe, producing

HEY, KIDS! Mum is now offering puppetry classes for kids. Classes for 3- to 5-year-olds (in collaboration with parents) focus on basic movement, story-based activities, and self-expression in what is basically pre-puppetry. Short- and longer-term (10-week) programs are available. Classes for youths 7–13 teach basic puppet manipulation and mask-making. Most of these classes are in 10-week sessions. Teens may join the 10-week evening classes for adults, provided they have a recommendation from a teacher and approval from Mum. Class offerings are slated to expand in coming years.

115 Arch St.

 $10–$24

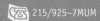 215/925-7MUM

 Sept–June, T–F 10, Sa–Su, 12, 2, and some shows 8

 Varies by performance

artistic director at Mum, "a puppet is any object we choose to give life to." The resultant living, breathing puppets can do a lot of things humans can't. They appear in a range of productions, from the occasional classic like the *Velveteen Rabbit* to *The Adventures of a Boy and His Dog on the High Seas* (a chapter in the continuing saga of, you guessed it, a boy and his dog) to *Revenge of the Fantoccini*, the "annual closet cleaning of new works" that's part of the Philadelphia Fringe Festival.

Shows at Mum's 85-seat black-box theater are not all for kids. A typical five-production season (each three to four weeks) might have three plays for all ages, one for the 10-and-up crowd, and one for high school and older, and might include visiting artists. Mum hopes to increase its school-year season to seven productions and to host a summer puppet festival by 2002. Like their audience, the puppets are having a growth spurt.

KEEP IN MIND
Book ahead for the often-packed performances, but if you don't catch a full-length show at the theater, watch out for other Mum appearances. You might find a puppet popping up with the Philadelphia Orchestra or appearing one weekend at the Please Touch Museum. Call Mum for a schedule.

EATS FOR KIDS **Food Tek** (22 S. 2nd St., tel. 215/238–1115) bills itself as a gourmet deli, and that pretty much sums it up. Walk past the deli counter to the booths and tables, and order regular deli sandwiches, salads, French baguette subs, pita pockets and pizzas, vegetarian items, and other concoctions for adults and adventurous kids (e.g., smoked turkey with sun-dried tomatoes, tavern ham with hot pepper cheese). For other local eateries, see listings for nearby attractions such as the Arden Children's Theatre, Betsy Ross House, Fireman's Hall, Franklin Court, and the National Liberty Museum.

MÜTTER MUSEUM

Conjoined twins, a murderer's brain, dwarf and giant skeletons: What more could a kid want? This anatomical, pathological, and medical-history museum, named not for the German word for mother but for the surgery professor whose specimen collection started it all, is not for every kid, though. Some people—mostly adults, actually—find double-meaning in the term "gross anatomy" and don't enjoy the Mütter. More's the pity, because they're missing out on an interesting and fun find.

Enter through the exhibit gallery, currently documenting infectious diseases around the world. You can check out micrographs of various infections, get tips on how to keep your kitchen germ-free, and learn about famous epidemics, including that Philly favorite, Legionnaires' Disease. This will get you in a suitable mood for the main event: the Mütter Museum itself.

Two floors contain display cases filled with bones and bottles. With the exception of

EATS FOR KIDS Many good, reasonably priced eateries are nearby: **T.A. Flannery's** (11 S. 21st St., tel. 215/561–1193), an Irish pub with great burgers; **Tony's** (17 S. 21st St., tel. 215/972–8203), for hoagies and steaks; and **Skyline Pizza** (2102 Market St., tel. 215/567–3294).

KEEP IN MIND Only you will know whether your kids (or you) are too squeamish for this museum. It's not too likely, though. There's something about the orderly displays, set in a wood and brass enclave inside the College of Physicians of Philadelphia, that goes a long way toward sanitizing the subject matter and making you feel comfortable staring. "If the adults can handle it, the kids can handle it," says museum director Gretchen Worden. And if your family really gets in the Mütter spirit, you can pick up a copy of the museum calendar to truly preserve the experience.

19 S. 22nd St.

 215/563-3737

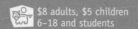 $8 adults, $5 children
6–18 and students

 M–Sa 10–4, Su 12–4

 7 and up

the exhibit on skin diseases, which are mostly models, the stuff here is real: That's someone's real mega-colon (no wonder he was constipated!) and a real fetus with 46 twists in the umbilical cord. Each skull on a wall of skulls is identified by name, age, occupation, and cause of death, leading you to wonder if there's something different about the skulls of a suicide and a pneumonia victim. Quite a bit of display space is given over to conjoined (a.k.a. Siamese) twins, including memorabilia, articles, photos, and a post-autopsy cast of Chang and Eng (the most famous conjoined twins) and their preserved shared liver. Kids too squeamish to stare into jars of formaldehyde can open drawers with more than 2,000 items that were swallowed or inhaled: jewelry, safety pins, dentures, bullets. . . even a skate key.

There's a lot to be learned here about the history of medicine and how people have approached anatomy and abnormality over the years. Kids who are into science and into finding out how things—in this case, their bodies—work, will like the museum. Kids who are into anything gross will love it.

HEY, KIDS! "I had a little bird, and it's name was Enza. I opened the window, and in-flew-Enza." This was a jump rope song in 1918, at the time of a worldwide Spanish flu (short for influenza) epidemic that killed 22 million people, including 500,000 in the United States. Imagine singing a jump rope song about cancer or AIDS! Sometimes people react to something scary by making a joke out of it. Do you ever do that?

NATIONAL LIBERTY MUSEUM

I f you're looking for fun and games, look elsewhere; but if you're looking for powerful, sobering, and important issues for your kids to ponder, look no further. Like traditional Philly historic-area sights, this new attraction is devoted to liberty. However, instead of concerning itself with the white, Protestant Founding Fathers, this unusual museum concentrates on heroes of all ages, races, religions, and nationalities and encourages thought about the sacrifices and vigilance that liberty sometimes requires.

There's a curious mix of items and concepts here, the most obvious being the combination of descriptive exhibits and art, representing media from glass to jelly beans. The many glass pieces—including the impressive, multistory *Flame of Liberty*, by Dale Chihuly—are meant to signify the fragility of liberty. Though this symbolism may be lost on kids, they might still think the stuff's cool.

While the ground floor treats America's diversity and the third floor deals with biblical

EATS FOR KIDS After visiting a museum dedicated to diversity, why not try a local ethnic restaurant? The well-respected **Mexican Post** (104 Chestnut St., tel. 215/923–5233) and **Shivnanda** (114 Chestnut St., tel. 215/925–1444), serving pretty mild Indian food, are both open lunch and dinner. If your kids' palates run to Brazilian, Japanese, Middle Eastern, or Afghani, just walk down Chestnut toward Front and take your pick. (Some restaurants are open for dinner only.) For good true-blue American fare, such as eggs, pancakes, sandwiches, and burgers, sit at the counter booths of **Mrs. K's Koffee Shop** (4th and Chestnut Sts., tel. 215/627–7991), breakfast and lunch only.

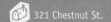 321 Chestnut St.

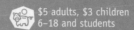 $5 adults, $3 children
6–18 and students

 Tu–S 10–5

 215/925-2800

 7 and up

themes, it's the second floor that invites the most thought and emotion. The north side honors heroes worldwide, many from World War II, whereas the southern half concerns violence in America. This exhibit can and should be shocking for parents and children (don't be surprised if you walk through wordlessly), though unfortunately many kids are inured to violence. In fact, reducing kids' exposure to violence is a key message. Unbelievable facts—such as that the average child witnesses 8,000 murders on TV before leaving elementary school—are coupled with messages of hope and suggestions on how kids can resolve conflicts peacefully and be heroes themselves. Perhaps the most moving exhibit is a simple paper shredder. Kids can write down hurtful things they have been called or have called others, and then shred them. According to museum founder Irvin Borowsky, children can sometimes be seen writing and shredding, with tears streaming down their face. It's a cathartic experience emblematic of this sometimes disturbing, often affirming museum.

KEEP IN MIND

Consider your children's dispositions before visiting the American violence exhibit. Though the intended path takes you From Conflict to Harmony, traveling backward and seeing only the second half avoids the most disturbing displays. Discussing violence beforehand helps; talking afterward is healthy and inevitable.

HEY, KIDS! Like other recently opened museums, this one has high-tech, interactive exhibits. Cast your electronic ballot at a voting machine or call up the stories of famous immigrants on touch screens. Lower-techies can "mail" words of hope, most of which are posted weekly. Go beyond the hands-on activities and check out the awesome hands-off artworks. Many are really cool, not only to look at but also to think about. The statue of John Lennon—a member of the Beatles (a rock group your parents probably liked) and champion of peace—is made of melted-down handguns. How cool is that?

NATIONAL TOY TRAIN MUSEUM

Lancaster County, known for buggies and other horse-drawn vehicles, seems like an odd place to find a mecca for iron-horse enthusiasts. Nevertheless, in the small hamlet of Strasburg, you can not only ride, clamber over, and sleep in trains, but you can make them run, too. This recently expanded and renovated museum, headquarters of the Train Collectors Association, is home to five big operating layouts and countless toy locomotives and cars on display.

Because it's operated by the collectors' association, the museum takes its collection seriously, catering to adult hobbyists. Toy trains on view represent the 1800s to the present, and an entire section of the museum is devoted to trains from before World War II. The variety here is impressive—from an alcohol-burning live steam locomotive circa 1840 to a little tin floor toy, from a Hubley cast-iron wind-up train circa 1890 to a Marklin Victorian station accessory from the early 20th century that is probably worth about six figures.

EATS FOR KIDS **Hershey Farm** (Rte. 896, tel. 717/687–8635) serves farm-fresh Pennsylvania Dutch cooking, both from a menu and in a popular local smorgasbord. For other Strasburg eateries, see the Railroad Museum of Pennsylvania.

HEY, KIDS! Sometimes it seems like the names of train gauges are just alphabet soup. From smallest to largest, they are Z, N, HO, S, O, G, and standard. HO is half the size of O, hence the initials, but most of the other letters are a mystery. Different manufacturers developed different sizes in the 1890s, and they never managed to merge them to a standard gauge (not to be confused with the gauge that's called "standard gauge"). G, sometimes referred to as 1 gauge, is popular for indoor-outdoor railroads used in garden layouts, and O is approximately 1/48 full size.

 Paradise La., Strasburg

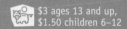 $3 ages 13 and up,
$1.50 children 6–12

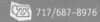 717/687–8976

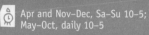 Apr and Nov–Dec, Sa–Su 10–5;
May–Oct, daily 10–5

 2–12

The highlights for most kids, however, are the operating electric train layouts, which are built and maintained by volunteers. Five layouts, each representing a different gauge—HO, S, O, G, and standard—can be set in motion by pushing buttons, sending trains barreling forward (reverse units have been disconnected) through varied landscapes: towns, farms, mountains, bridges, water towers, and windmills included. Some accessories are modern; others have been around for decades, like Lionel's papier-mâché mountains (1920s) in the standard-gauge layout. Each gauge also has an adjacent display of same-size rolling stock; little kids find Thomas, Annie, and Clarabel in no time. At Christmas, the layouts are decorated with Santas and reindeer, but afterward, when the museum is closed for the winter, some of them are given makeovers.

When you've had enough of little trains, be sure to see the *big* trains not far away at the Railroad Museum of Pennsylvania (*see below*).

GETTING THERE From the Pennsylvania Turnpike or the Schuylkill Expressway, take U.S. 202 south to U.S. 30 west. Past Soudersburg, turn left onto Ronks Road. (Alternately, stay on the turnpike to Exit 21. Take U.S. 222 south to Lancaster and U.S. 30 east, and turn right on Ronks Road.) Where Ronks forks into Fairview Lane and Paradise Lane, stay to the left. The museum is on your left, next to—what else in Strasburg—a motel of cabooses. Continuing on Paradise Lane brings you to Route 741. Turn right to reach the railroad, the railroad museum, and Strasburg proper.

NEW HOPE & IVYLAND RAILROAD

When the whistle blows, Old Number 40, a black 1925 Baldwin steam locomotive (or a diesel friend), departs on another 50-minute excursion into the Bucks County countryside. You, meanwhile, are tucked inside one of the authentic 1920s Reading coaches, some of which still have mahogany interiors, cloth seats, old signage ("Spitting is Prohibited"), and old windows. (Leave the windows alone, as they can slam shut and hurt little fingers.)

A narrator tells stories about what you see out the window: the trestle where poor Pauline was tied to the tracks in the silent movie series *The Perils of Pauline,* and an old stone house that was once a stop on a railroad of another kind, the Underground Railroad. Much of the narration is lost on small kids, who are busy chattering away, staring out at nothing in particular, imagining themselves as engineers, or, by the time you return, dozing contentedly on your shoulder (50 minutes is plenty for wee ones). The 9-mile round-trip goes as far as Lahaska, where the engine needs 10 minutes to complete its run around,

KEEP IN MIND In summer, 1½-hour trips are also offered from Warminster to Wycombe, but they're not as scenic. Depending on where you live, there might be a closer train trip: the Wilmington & Western Railroad (2301 Newport Gap Pike, Wilmington, DE, tel. 302/998–1930) or Lancaster County's Strasburg Rail Road (Rte. 741, tel. 717/687–7522). For different vintage transportation in New Hope, try the mule-drawn barges of the New Hope Canal Boat Company (149 S. Main St., tel. 215/862–0758), April–October. (Incidentally, if you won't be in New Hope long, it's cheaper to park at street meters than at the station.)

unhooking itself and coming around to the rear (now front) to start pulling the other way. Wave to the engineer as the locomotive passes.

On summer Tuesdays and Thursdays, one coach plays host to the Song & Story Hour, good for the Thomas-loving crowd. A banjo-strumming storyteller clad in overalls and engineer's cap recounts the bravery of Old Number 40, back when it was Young Number 40 and it saved a big Streamliner. Everyone is encouraged to sing and shout along and engage in some make-believe.

Other special trains include a fall and spring Train Robbery, during which Bonnie and Clyde might rob you, if you bought play money at the station by donating to charity. Fall is also foliage season. By November, the North Pole Express takes 1½-hour trip to Buckingham, during which Santa listens to every child's wish list. Don't be surprised if a toy train is on it.

HEY, KIDS! Old Number 40 weighs 176,000 pounds, and its tender carries 8 tons of coal and 6,000 gallons of water. The fireman needs to shovel more than ½ ton of coal to get you to Lahaska and back. Think you'd like to do that?

EATS FOR KIDS Friendly **Villa Vito Restaurant** (26 W. Bridge St., tel. 215/862–9936) turns out all sorts of pizza, other Italian specials, and sandwiches. **Bridge Street Café** (37 W. Bridge St., tel. 215/862–4485) is a small deli with build-your-own hoagies and deli sandwiches along with such sandwiches as the Sloppy Sue and the good old PB&J for $1.95. It even has a jukebox. **El Taco Loco** (6 Stockton Ave., tel. 215/862–0908) could be called El Taco Locomotive since it fronts on the railroad tracks; order Mexican at the counter, and eat at indoor tables.

NEW JERSEY STATE AQUARIUM
& CAMDEN CHILDREN'S GARDEN

When Camden's aquarium opened in the early 1990s, it became known for having a lot of local, brown fish. Today, however, this top-notch attraction combines an aquarium and interactive children's garden, education and entertainment, and fish spanning the spectrum and the seas.

You can't help but walk through the lushly planted children's garden, part playground and part horticultural lesson. There's a butterfly garden; a picnic garden, where vegetables grow; a dinosaur garden, home to a sculptural apatosaurus in a waterfall and a sandy dig pit; and even a Secret Garden, part of a corner where storybook scenes come alive. Stand in the Tree House and survey the whole area.

Next, journey to the wet and wild side, stopping by the penguins and seals on your way indoors. Check your map for show times; seal behavior demonstrations are fun and informative, and besides, those harbor seals are just so darn cute.

KEEP IN MIND Ocean Quest, is a four-part motion-simulator submarine adventure. Accommodating 100 people, it takes 30 minutes from briefing room through elevator tunnel to the actual theater ride. Some adjustment to the voyage's intensity can be made for individuals with various restrictions.

EATS FOR KIDS On site, you'll find only fast food, available from a few snack stands and the **Riverview Café.** This indoor cafeteria serves the usual—burgers, hot dogs, chicken, and yes, even fish fillets (don't worry, they're not aquarium castoffs)—but has a wonderful view of the river and Philadelphia skyline from its outdoor deck. Across the street, the **Crossroads Café** (2 Riverside Dr., tel. 856/365–1770) has reasonably priced sandwiches, salads, and gourmet pizza (plus breakfast), but it's not open for dinner or on weekends. In summer, however, it has a weekend barbecue outside, where there's usually also a hot dog cart.

 1 Riverside Dr., Camden, NJ

 856/365–3300 or 800/616–JAWS aquarium, 856/365–TREE children's garden

 Aquarium and garden $12.95 ages 12 and up, $11.45 students, $9.95 children 3–11; garden only $5 ages 12 and up, $3 children

Mid-Apr–mid-Sept, daily 9:30–5:30; mid-Sept–mid-Apr, M–F 9:30–4:30, Sa–Su 10–5

 2 and up

In the less cute department are the sharks: little sharks (and stingrays) in the Shark Zone touch tank and big, beady-eyed sand tiger and sand bar sharks in the 760,000-gallon Open Ocean Tank. They, along with giant stingrays, sea turtles, and dozens of other fish species, circle the tank in slow motion. Dive Shows and Tank Talks occur throughout the day, as do performances of the Drama Gills Family Theatre.

The aquarium doesn't have many knobs and buttons, but it hardly matters. The allure is the variety of aquatic animals—more than 4,000 representing some 500 species. Exhibits range from the dark black-lit depths, where eerie moray eels peer out of tubes and moon jellies float in a purple ocean, to a bright circular coral reef. The C.O.O.L. (Conservation Outreach and Observation Lab) exhibit uses not only fish, amphibians, and reptiles, but also insects, birds (toucans and helmeted curassows), and a mammal (the coypu) to teach about global conservation. It's the aquarium's latest effort to mix a little learning and a lot of water to create something for just about everyone.

HEY, KIDS! For the best chances of touching a shark, keep your hands away from the edge. If you hang over, the shark will see your shadow and stay away. After its eyes pass, quickly try to touch its back—gently, with two fingers. If you're lucky, you'll get a brief feel of rough skin, but there's no guarantee. Despite a tiny brain, these sharks aren't stupid; they usually swim deep near the edges where visitors stand. So if you can't reach deep enough, even when standing on the tank's small step, visit the upstairs touch tank, where starfish and sea urchins hold still.

PENNSBURY MANOR

Around Philadelphia, if the answer to a history question isn't Benjamin Franklin, it's probably William Penn. In 1681, Penn received a charter for Pennsylvania (translation: Penn's woods) and founded the colony based on principles of religious tolerance and ethnic diversity. He dealt fairly with the area's Lenni Lenape Indians and planned Philadelphia (translation: city of brotherly love), where he lived in winter. Pennsbury Manor was Penn's summer home, or, more accurately, the site of his home. The structure that stands here today is a New Deal–era reconstruction that conveys the spirit, if not the exact details, of the original. Interestingly, Penn spent only a few years at Pennsbury before returning to England, but a walk around this quiet estate on the banks of the Delaware reveals why he often wished he were here.

Though you can wander the grounds on your own, to enter the buildings you'll have to take an approximately 1½-hour guided tour. Tours start with a 15-minute orientation video in the modern visitor center and then concentrate on the Manor House. Guides try to tailor

HEY, KIDS! Oh, those wacky Penns (and others like them)! They put rugs on tables, not floors (to keep them clean), pressed creases *into* tablecloths for parties, and slept partially sitting up in case the devil came to call. Their medicine? Hot cups applied to skin created blisters and brought bad blood to the surface, while pomander balls (dried oranges with spices) helped the nose—by masking body odor. As for food and drink, Penn's beloved hot chocolate was the equivalent of two melted candy bars, and the greatest dinner delicacy, bestowed on the guest of honor, was the main dish's eyeballs.

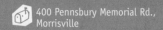

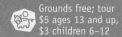
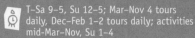

the tour somewhat if kids are present, but small children will just have to endure a certain amount of typical furnishings talk. Encourage them to listen for stories that tell something about the man and his times.

Outbuildings show even more of day-to-day life. The Bake and Brew House was the place for cooking, baking, and beer brewing. (Even kids as young as 3 drank beer, as water was unsafe.) Visit the barn and look for resident animals, similar to those that lived here in Penn's day. If you come on Sunday, you can watch as costumed interpreters demonstrate a 17th-century activity, such as open-hearth cooking, trades like blacksmithing or carpentry, or even sheep shearing. Some Sundays bring living-history theater, when you can join the interpreters in acting out a scene—from pub games and gossip to a witch trial—and bring the 17th century to life.

EATS FOR KIDS

U.S. 13 has two diners: **Golden Eagle** (300 Bath Rd., at U.S. 13, Bristol, tel. 215/785–6926) and **Dallas Diner** (7025 U.S. 13, Levittown, tel. 215/547–0990). The **King George II Inn** (102 Radcliffe St., Bristol, tel. 215/788–5536) has a river view. Also see Sesame Place.

GETTING THERE Penn's country estate is 26 miles from Philadelphia. To get here, he was rowed five hours on the Delaware in a barge (the trip by horse took 1½ days). You don't have that option. Take I-95 north to Route 413 south to U.S. 13 north. Cross the Pennsylvania Turnpike (there's an exit here) and turn right at the next light, Green Lane. Where it ends, turn left on Radcliffe Street, which changes to Main Street and then Bordentown Road. After 4½ miles, turn right on Pennsbury Memorial Road. A huge landfill here might have Penn rolling in his English grave.

PENNSYLVANIA ACADEMY OF THE FINE ARTS

This is not your typical art museum, with rectangular rooms and plain white walls. Walls at PAFA are decorated with carved stone and gold leaf and painted in rich hues like red, green, and taupe. Floors are embellished with tile mosaics, and ceilings are painted a deep blue with stars. The real star, though, is the High Victorian Gothic building itself, designed by local architects Frank Furness and George Hewitt. Restored to its original splendor, it gives kids a lot to look at.

And then there's the art, most of it oil paintings and sculpture and all of it American, with an emphasis on the local. If you're so inclined, you can trace the course of American history through the artwork—from portraits of America's Founding Fathers to landscapes of westward expansion. Works from the 20th century add brighter colors and more impressionistic styles. The scale is manageable enough that you can see the whole museum in an hour.

KEEP IN MIND Saturdays at 11, PAFA offers family programs that are free with admission. Some take in exhibits, others are purely studio experiences, and one program a month also has a performance component. Examples of previous programs are "19th-Century Animation" and "Try Your Hand at Printmaking." Sounds fun, no?

EATS FOR KIDS The **Museum Café** (tel. 215/972–2058) is basically a nice cafeteria offering bagels and muffins for breakfast and sandwiches, salad, and soup for lunch. **Reading Terminal Market** (12th St., between Filbert and Arch Sts., tel. 215/922–2317) is an indoor bazaar and a Philly institution. Roam the stalls—from produce stands to Pennsylvania Dutch pretzel booths—and pick what you want: a sandwich, cheese steak, taco, gyro, Chinese food, and the finale: ice cream from Bassett's. Kids like "feeding" Philbert, a big piggy bank that collects money for charity. Also see Chinatown and City Hall.

118 N. Broad St.

 215/972-7600

$5 adults, $3 children
5-18; Su 3-5 free

T-Sa 10-5, Su 11-5

5 and up

Young children might well get bored here, but peppering your visit with stories and games can help. While looking at the two enormous paintings flanking the staircase, imagine how people used to view them, as entertainment. People would sit before a drawn curtain, as we do before a play, and the painting would be dramatically unveiled. Today's entertainment lies in searching for items—as in a hidden picture puzzle—in Benjamin West's *Death on a Pale Horse*. Children unimpressed by realistic landscapes and formal portraits should head to Gallery 9, home to very different landscapes and portraits, such as the vivid blue and purple skyline that is *Philadelphia* and *Wee Maureen,* a simple girl with piercing blue eyes.

For real fun and games, go to the Family Resource Center in the Rotunda. Handouts let kids color famous pictures (crayons provided) or draw their own, fill out worksheets, or do word searches and puzzles. Or they can build with blocks or put together puzzles representing artworks in the collection. They may even temporarily forget they're in an art museum.

HEY, KIDS!   Compare the portraits of George Washington, both by famous painters. Why might he look different? *George Washington at Princeton*, done by Charles Willson Peale in 1779, depicts Gen. Washington in battle. Gilbert Stuart's painting (1796), shows Washington the president. Stuart's portraits of Washington, including the one on the $1 bill, are so famous that they shape our view of what George really looked like. (Remember: They had no cameras then.) No wonder one child said about Peale's portrait, "That's not George Washington."

PEOPLE'S LIGHT & THEATRE COMPANY
FAMILY DISCOVERY SERIES

Words like "innovative" and "creative" are generally overused when referring to children's theater. Words like "provocative" and "challenging" seldom are. But this three-production season of new plays and new adaptations of classics tends to be all these things.

Plays here are not mere entertainment. Costumes or scenery may be simple, but the issues tackled are complex and not easily summed up with a happy ending or Aesop-style moral. A typical season, for example, included a musical adaptation of *A Christmas Carol; The Music Lesson,* a time-shifting tale of war and memory as told through two music teachers and two students, a Bosnian prodigy and an angry American girl; and *The Thoughts and Travels of Nicki,* with a cast that included not only the aforementioned little girl but also a monster, sly cat, flying horse, unicycling bear, and a troupe of jugglers. Without crossing the line into overly depressing or heavy-handed territory, productions deal with questions affecting today's kids, such as fitting in or a parent's death. Even

HEY, KIDS! Most shows raise a lot of questions. Luckily, after most performances, the cast and other behind-the-scenes people come out onstage to give you a lot of answers. These are called Talkback sessions, because it's your turn to do the talking. Don't be nervous. No question is bad or wrong. Maybe you'd like to know how they make snow or some other effect, how the actors learned an accent, or how they feel about their character. Perhaps you didn't understand something in the play and would like it clarified. The actors really enjoy these little chats, and you probably will, too.

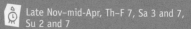 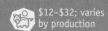

 39 Conestoga Rd., Malvern

$12–$32; varies by production

610/647–1900

Late Nov–mid-Apr, Th–F 7, Sa 3 and 7, Su 2 and 7

Varies by production

more appropriately, they *raise* questions, since provoking thought and discussion is one of the series's missions. This can happen either in the 10- to 15-minute Talkback sessions that follow performances or around the dinner table at home. Family discovery is taken seriously.

Performances are given either on the Main Stage (mostly proscenium and delta configurations) or the smaller Steinbright Stage (black box). Staging and costumes vary from the elaborate to the understated; sometimes all an actor uses to change from one character to another is the addition of a red sash or turban. The excellent actors—from People's Light's resident company as well as visiting artists—are trained in and incorporate lots of movement. Get ready for them to climb on as well as around the set. In fact, get ready for anything.

GETTING THERE From the Schuylkill Expressway westbound, get off onto U.S. 202 south. Exit at Route 401, Frazer. Turn left, and follow Route 401 east for about 1¼ miles. The theater will be on your left.

EATS FOR KIDS Though **Places!** (tel. 610/647–8060), in the theater's adjacent farmhouse building, is an upscale bistro, it's casual enough so that children feel comfortable. Open for lunch and dinner (dinner is more expensive), it has the requisite kids' menu and coloring packet. Within five minutes of the theater are **King Street Grille & Market** (400 E. King St., tel. 610/644–2644), serving breakfast and lunch; the **Classic Diner** (352 Lancaster Ave., tel. 610/725–0515); and **Basil Restaurant** (U.S. 30 and King St., Paoli, tel. 610/647–1500), which also has bistro fare.

THE PEOPLE'S PLACE

It's a dilemma. How do you learn about the Amish and Mennonites of Lancaster County—and there are 20 or 30 such groups within 20 miles of Intercourse—without prying into their very private lives? One answer is this tasteful interpretive center, combining a half-hour documentary and a walk-through museum. The approach is straightforward; yet it comes with a warning not to oversimplify these people and the acknowledgment that, with only an hour or two, to do so is inevitable.

The museum, called 20Q (for 20 questions), asks and answers frequently asked questions about the Amish and Mennonites (divided instead into Old Order and Modern groups). For example, it explains why most Old Order groups wear plain-color clothes that cover the entire body (for decorum and nonconformity) and why they drive buggies instead of cars (they believe machines separate people from one another). Fittingly, except for some recordings, exhibits are pretty low-tech and are augmented by carved-wood scenes of Amish life.

KEEP IN MIND Lancaster County has plenty of Amish-theme attractions, though many have a commercial feel that undercuts their message. Options include buggy rides and re-created Amish houses. Remember, however, that the Amish do not self-interpret, so you won't hear the story of the Amish from the Amish themselves.

EATS FOR KIDS It would be a shame to come to Lancaster County and not sample such classic Pennsylvania Dutch cuisine as ham loaf, fresh sausage, chow-chow, and shoofly pie. To eat family-style in a country farmhouse atmosphere, nip down to **Stoltzfus Farm Restaurant** (Rte. 772 East, tel. 717/768–8156). It's open Monday–Saturday May–October and weekends in April and November, but is closed completely December–March. If you'd rather order from a menu or pile your plate at a buffet, drive a few miles west to the diner that is the **Bird-in-Hand Family Restaurant** (Rte. 340, Bird-in-Hand, tel. 717/768–8266).

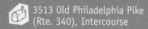 3513 Old Philadelphia Pike
(Rte. 340), Intercourse

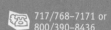 717/768–7171 or
800/390–8436

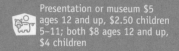 Presentation or museum $5
ages 12 and up, $2.50 children
5–11; both $8 ages 12 and up,
$4 children

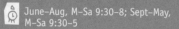 June–Aug, M–Sa 9:30–8; Sept–May,
M–Sa 9:30–5

 5 and up

Young kids may tire of pondering questions, but child-friendly activities keep them from getting too far ahead of you. Kids can pick up Plain Pig's Alphabet and identify 26 Amish-related items in viewfinders. They can don plain clothes and hats, sit in a schoolroom with exercises from an Amish schoolbook, play with a wooden barn, hunt for Menno (founder of the Mennonites) in a "Where's Menno?" picture, or climb in a buggy box and pretend to signal.

The three-screen slide presentation, *Who Are the Amish?,* covers similar territory. Young kids may not understand the concepts, but they'll probably like the song about animals, about midway through. A brief question-and-answer period follows.

Though the People's Place provides plenty of facts, the biggest lessons here are about insight, not information. We are reminded to keep an open mind and see complexity in all people. Kids tend to focus on differences between themselves and the Amish, but they hopefully gain interest in and respect for these peaceful, spiritual people.

HEY, KIDS! According to the Amish, we English (the Amish name for outsiders, even though most of us aren't from England) think we're saving time by using cars instead of buggies. In reality, though, everyone has the same amount of time. Some people just spend more of it getting places. Why not try thinking like that, and enjoy your driving time? Without staring, watch out for farmers plowing behind horses, windmills, silos, solid-color laundry hanging on lines, rolling cornfields, and, of course, buggies. Amish buggies have gray tops; Mennonites' are black. And whatever you do, don't ask "Are we there yet?"

PHILADELPHIA INSECTARIUM

Years ago, an exterminating company put its "catch of the day" in a window display for all to see. Its popularity led to the creation of this weird and wonderful all-insect museum that's well worth a trip to Northeast Philly.

The museum itself occupies floors two and three above the office and gift shop, where you purchase your tickets. The second floor is given over *mostly* to inanimate displays and interactive exhibits, including dress-up costumes, a scale that weighs you in bugs (56,999 grasshoppers or so for the average 4th grader), and Q&A columns that buzz when you nail the bug lore. Specimens under glass range from iridescent beetles to mantids, from the aptly named *Zurycantha horrida* (a long, prickly brown thing from New Guinea) to a huge collection of butterflies and moths lining the walls. Representing 98% of North American species, they were donated by an avid collector. A key animate exception is the cockroach kitchen/bathroom. Behind a 5-foot wall of glass stands a kitchenette crawling with an uncountable number of American cockroaches. They sustain themselves (as roaches have

HEY, KIDS! The Insectarium welcomes all arthropods, not just six-legged ones. "Arthur who?" you ask. Arthropods are a broad animal group that includes insects, arachnids (spiders and scorpions), centipedes, and millipedes. You probably thought that centipedes and millipedes were close cousins. Actually, they're more distantly related than are dragonflies and dung beetles. Centipedes, which have flat bodies and one pair of legs per body segment, are carnivores (some even eat snakes), while millipedes, with round bodies and two leg pairs per segment, are vegetarians. Think more feet make millipedes faster? Think again. Ask an educator to show you how fast they both move.

for 320 million years), eating the carcasses of their forebears and leftovers periodically tossed in by staff, laying egg cases (what look like black Tic Tacs), and scurrying out of the cabinets when an educator squirts the counter with water. There's no denying that they're gross, but they're also pretty interesting.

The colorful third floor is almost completely given over to live specimens. Here you'll see terrariums and aquariums filled with well-camouflaged walking sticks, large diving beetles that do a brisk beetle paddle, and even tarantulas and a black widow spider. This is also the place to hold bugs: a Madagascar hissing cockroach; the scorpion-like vinegaroon, whose name comes from the smelly substance it secretes when scared (don't worry: they're generally used to people enough not to hiss or secrete, respectively); or a southwestern millipede, whose feet some kids think feel like Velcro. Even squeamish kids become confirmed bug-o-philes.

EATS FOR KIDS

If those yummy, crunchy, cheese- or barbecue-coated Larvets (mealworms)—often for sale in the gift shop—don't fill you up, have a picnic in the new herb-scented bug-sanctuary garden outside. The **Dining Car** (8826 Frankford Ave., tel. 215/338-5113) is a wonderful, clean diner.

KEEP IN MIND

Okay, so you might initially be put off. You might even think you've journeyed to an exterminator's instead of a museum. Phone calls here are answered "Steve's Bug Off," the museum's parent company, whose sign out front is actually much more prominent than the door marked "Insectarium." And then there are all those "icky" bugs. Get over it! Your kids probably will faster than you do. Educators here dispel myths and teach interesting insect info, including the fact that every creature is useful. Even termites help by ridding forests of rotting trees. Besides, sometimes it's fun to be grossed out.

PHILADELPHIA MUSEUM OF ART

Children, it would seem, are born with museum feet rather than museum eyes, but visiting this vast treasure trove can start them on the road to becoming bona fide art lovers. The trick to keeping youngsters interested is to keep it short, keep it varied, and keep it moving. Thankfully, there's so much to see—over 300,000 objects in 600,000 square feet—that you can see a *lot* and still leave plenty for subsequent trips.

Pick up one of the self-guiding Family Tours, brief themed tours (five or six artworks) with worksheets (use pencil; pens aren't allowed in the museum). Your child may not want to fill out the pages right then, but they're good for pointing out kid-friendly approaches to kid-friendly pieces.

A favorite tour is Arms and Armor. Here older children might ponder the relative merits of armor versus chain mail or compare an early helmet (600–400 BC) to elaborate gilded armor (probably worn by Maximilian II, Holy Roman Emperor 1564–1576). Youngsters

EATS FOR KIDS

The upscale **Cafeteria** (relax: it has hot dogs) is better for kids than the **Restaurant** (tel. 215/684–7990). The **Café Flower Shop** (2501 Meredith St., at 25th St., tel. 215/232–1076) has weekend brunch and Wednesday–Friday lunch (sandwiches, salads) amid greenery that's for sale.

KEEP IN MIND Sunday morning is a great time to come with kids. For one thing, admission before 1 is free. For another, special family programs are offered, many of which have both gallery time and studio time, so your newly inspired kids can express themselves. (Programs with studio sessions cost $3 per child, free for parents.) Frequent special family events include performances by guest artists, hands-on workshops, and family tours. If you do come on a Sunday morning, however, come at 10; by 11:30, it can get crowded, as you won't be the only ones attracted by free admission.

26th St. and Benjamin Franklin Pkwy.

 $8 adults, $5 children
5–18 and students;
Su 10–1 free

T and Th–Su 10–5, W 10–8:45

215/763–8100 voice,
215/684–7500 recording

 3 and up

can imagine getting hot and heavy in a jousting suit while riding an armored horse.

Over in Asia, a Chinese palace hall stands adjacent to a Japanese ceremonial teahouse. Some kids prefer the ornate palace room, with its throne and dog cage, while others like the simpler teahouse in its bamboo garden. Wander through 19th-century Europe to Gallery 161. Children usually gravitate to the coin-laden fountain, but do pause at Monet's footbridge and Van Gogh's *Sunflowers* before passing from the sublime to the ridiculous: the modern art galleries. Okay, this *is* serious art, but it's hard not to smirk at Robert Gober's sink with legs (inexplicably two left feet) protruding where the faucets should be. Representing the likes of Pollock, Warhol, Duchamp, and Rothko, the collection is kid-accessible (though not always kid-appropriate—watch for occasional graphic subject matter). Perhaps it's the allure of big, bright canvases or the imaginative possibilities in abstract art. Or perhaps, as many parents assert, it's that the art is similar to children's own creations. Regardless, this is a great place for kids to think about art and realize how much they like it.

HEY, KIDS! Part of the fun of contemporary art is that it can look different to different people. Some works can even look different depending on how you look at them. Try to find Chuck Close's painting *Paul*. Can you guess why it's called *Paul*? From far away, what do you see? Squint your eyes. Does he get clearer? Move closer, and you'll see that he's made of small, brightly colored shapes. Can you focus on the face and the shapes at the same time? So you see, there are many ways to look at art. And they're all fine.

PHILADELPHIA TROLLEY WORKS

18

When your Victorian "trolley" (actually a bus in trolley clothing) pulls away from the Liberty Bell, don't be surprised if your tour guide asks everyone on board where they're from. Don't be surprised either if not one person answers, "Philadelphia." This tour is a distinctly tourist thing to do. After all, why would Philadelphians want to ride around the city all day without having to worry about traffic, parking, or public transportation; listen to tour guides describe various and sundry city sights with the odd joke or anecdote thrown in; and get on and off at their leisure to sightsee on their own? Well, maybe they have some out-of-town friends visiting.

Trolleys leave every 30 minutes (20 minutes on weekends May through mid-October) from 5th and Market and take 1½ hours to complete the loop. Add to that an approximately 45-minute spur through Fairmount Park, generally covering either the East or West Park, which you can pick up at stop 9 for no extra charge. All told, you can easily make a day

HEY, KIDS! A lot, but not all, of the narration will be about how Philadelphia was a long time ago. According to guides, for example, except for Market Street (once High Street), east–west streets were named for trees. Many names, like Chestnut and Pine, remain, but Race Street actually used to be called Sassafras Street; it was rechristened not in honor of different ethnic groups but because a lot of horse races were held there. Can you imagine holding horse races on Race Street? It's about as easy as picturing a public hanging at Logan Circle, another narrator tidbit.

5th and Market Sts. and 19 other stops around the city

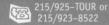 215/925-TOUR or 215/923-8522

 $18 ages 13 and up, $5 children 6–12; park only $10 ages 13 and up, $5 children

 Memorial Day–Labor Day, daily 9:30–6; early Sept–late May, daily 9:30–5:30

 3 and up

of it once you factor in a few visits to some classic Philly sights—from those in the historic district through Chinatown and Logan Circle, past Eastern State Penitentiary and the parkway museums (look to see if anyone is running up the art museum steps to pose like Rocky), to South Street and Penn's Landing, and back to the historic district. In fact, you can ride several loops if you wish, since your pass is for a full day, not just a circuit. (See separate listings for individual sights.)

Tour guides range from informative but dry to witty and engaging. If you're not getting much out of yours, exit at the next stop and catch a later trolley. Some guides will probably tell your kids, and you, a lot you didn't know about the city—some of it even accurate, though a grain or two of salt should be employed, as necessary.

EATS FOR KIDS

Since you can reboard repeatedly, eat wherever your family gets hungry. See restaurants under Old City, Center City, and Ben Franklin Parkway sights or eat on ebullient South Street, where **Johnny Rockets** (443 South St., tel. 215/829-9222) serves burgers with a side of synchronized dance.

KEEP IN MIND Okay, so this isn't a real Philadelphia trolley. Unfortunately, not many are left, at least compared to their heyday, when ⅔ of transit riders went by trolley. Today SEPTA trolley service is limited to the city's southwest (a subway-surface system) and a few suburban routes, but most cars date to the '80s. For a more vintage and child-friendly experience, hop aboard the shiny chrome and green 1930s-era trolley in the basement of SEPTA headquarters (1234 Market St., Trolley Works stop 8). Pay your invisible fare, chuckle at the old ads, and leave the driving to your child.

PHILADELPHIA ZOO

Dating to 1874, America's first zoo is rightfully proud of its pedigree. You can't help but notice its age, whether you're walking through the charming Victorian entrance or some older buildings, where bare cages do little to evoke the phrase "naturalistic habitat." These types of exhibits are fast becoming extinct, however. New and renovated facilities have made the zoo an undeniably fresh and visitor-friendly experience.

Lions and tigers and bears are all here, as are giraffes, zebras, elephants, and hippos. But these giants can't top the Primate Reserve, wonderfully redesigned after a tragic fire. Approach via the Lemur Trail, where you actually enter lemur habitat. If you're lucky, one will come near. Inside the air-conditioned building, you can watch langurs frolic amid cargo nets and hanging crates, blond and brunette gibbons swing from bamboo poles, and fluffy-tailed colobus monkeys cavort, their black and white fur fringed like a leather jacket. Outside, gorillas may groom and orangutans caper in their wonderland of old trees.

EATS FOR KIDS Zoo eateries are all of the fast-food cafeteria type. Some have indoor seating, and **Tiger Terrace** is open through the winter. There's also a picnic grove for the BYOP crowd, but please remember not to feed any people-food to the animals.

HEY, KIDS! For $3.50, you can buy a Talking Storybook key that unlocks tales about the zoo and its conservation efforts from solar-powered speakers. For example, you might learn that warthogs don't really have warts or that each zebra has a unique pattern of stripes (like our fingerprints). But you don't need a key to learn interesting things. Just keep your eyes peeled for signs with animal facts, like that when a new naked mole rat becomes queen, her body gets longer, or that the smell in the Carnivore House is tiger and lion urine used to mark territory, or that...

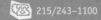

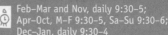

Purchase $1 worth of nectar, and various parrot species will alight on you at Parrot Paradise. It's a hoot (or is that a coo?), but be warned: They may eat the sweet treat, lick your face, or nibble your ear. A sink is located outside the exit; antiseptic is available if anyone's skin gets broken. Youngsters also like feeding barnyard animals in the Children's Zoo and scaling the treehouse. Docents at "Just Ask" carts let you touch real specimens, such as an elephant tooth or ear skin. Or rent a swan boat ($12) and paddle around Bird Lake.

The dimly lit herpetile house, home to reptiles and amphibians, brings you up close and personal (but not too personal) to some amazing creatures, like a green anaconda, poison dart frogs, and the vibrantly colored panther chameleon, whose independently moving eyes have added allure. Don't miss the playful penguins, giraffe-like okapi, or the new Pigs of the World exhibit. Come to think of it, though you won't want to miss anything, with 42 acres and dozens of daily events to cover, you'll have to.

KEEP IN MIND No two visits are alike. You could stand rapt while a river otter or polar bear swims gracefully, or stare expectantly at a dozing pile of wet fur. Animals are generally active early, so, for example, that's the likeliest time for a lemur to cross your path. Parrots don't watch the clock, however, even in hot weather, though they head south in winter. Some animals, especially African plains dwellers, are brought inside (and may not be visible) in cold weather. To ensure you'll see great action, pick up a map, which has the day's schedule, and attend a feeding and/or keeper talk.

PLEASE TOUCH MUSEUM

Where does the single-digit crowd go for an interactive experience they can relate to? They go, as have thousands of youngsters before them, to this well-loved institution whose name underscores its hands-on mission. Opened in 1976, the two-story museum fairly bursts at the seams with things for kids to wrap their hands and feet and developing minds around.

In the supermarket, kids race around with carts, grab boxes and cans off the shelves, and take them to the checkout. (Lest you think nothing changes, scanners have replaced the registers of the past.) The littlest children may do nothing more than pick up the fake foodstuffs and drop them on the floor, while their parents and enthusiastic schoolchildren gather up abandoned items and restock the shelves. If only kids were this compulsive at home!

Some other exhibits include the museum's mascot, Artie the Elephant, a big pachyderm sculpture made out of junk, and SEPTA Bus 1234 (well, the front section anyway), which

KEEP IN MIND PTM plans to open in the new Penn's Landing Family Entertainment Center in summer 2003, after a temporary closure. It will contain triple the exhibit space and will connect "experience zones" with the world outside. For example, the City Capers area, including streets, and the supermarket, will look out on Center City, while River Adventures will overlook the Delaware and its bridges. A carousel—the first to operate in Philadelphia since 1963—will include not only horses but also classic children's book characters. Don't worry: Artie will hop an improved bus to the new building, too.

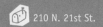 210 N. 21st St.

 $8.95 ages 1 and up

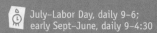 July–Labor Day, daily 9–6; early Sept–June, daily 9–4:30

215/963–0667

 1–9

has been headed to the Please Touch Museum for nearly a decade. Climb aboard to ride or drive. Still other second-floor areas are devoted to bringing *Alice in Wonderland* or the works of Maurice Sendak to life, letting kids broadcast the weather or news at Me on TV, or giving those 3 and under their own space, Barnyard Babies. The first floor, largely taken up by service/reception areas, also has a theater for special performances. As for the "museum" moniker, it is reflected in the collections of toys dating back to 1945, adding to parental nostalgia.

For the time being, the Please Touch Museum isn't a big, new, high-tech facility. It's a frequently crowded, well-used play place filled with activities as simple as a slide and plastic fruit and as complex as optical illusions. That will all change with construction of a new museum at Penn's Landing. What won't change is the museum's name and mission, which is a good thing, because touching is what its core audience does best.

EATS FOR KIDS
Little John's Pizza (161 N. 21st St., tel. 215/246–0653) has pizza, burgers, hoagies, salads, and so on. After the move, the museum will have a full-service restaurant. Also see the Academy of Natural Sciences, Franklin Institute, Mütter Museum, and, at Penn's Landing, the Independence Seaport Museum.

HEY, KIDS! If you've ever read or heard any of the stories represented here—like *Alice in Wonderland* or *Where the Wild Things Are*—try to figure out what part of the story each activity depicts. For example, why, when you paint the roses red in the Wonderland section, does a voice cackle "Off with their heads!"? And why, when you pull on a rope in the Sendak area, do trees grow out of the corners of Max's bed? If, on the other hand, you haven't read these books, maybe you should.

RAILROAD MUSEUM OF PENNSYLVANIA

Anyone who's ever played Monopoly knows about the Pennsylvania Railroad—at least that it costs $200. However, to really learn about that railway, its heyday in the late 19th and early 20th centuries—when 90% of intercity travelers went by train—and trains in general, you'll have to visit Pennsylvania's official railroad museum. Even if railroading history isn't your family's thing, you'll still marvel at the sight of the enormous hall filled with enormous rail cars, made even more real by the smell of creosote.

Over 100 engines and cars are preserved and displayed outside in the yard and inside in the impressive 100,000-square-foot Rolling Stock Hall. You might want to start by going up a story to the Observation Bridge, from which you can look down on a vast sea of black and red—locomotives, freight and passenger cars, and cabooses—and find the two yellow cars (a ventilator/refrigerator car and a very early combination baggage car/coach), at opposite ends of the hall.

KEEP IN MIND Though it's not always open, try to visit the Railway Education Center (donations accepted). Interactive exhibits include live-steam demonstrations, a display on trains in pop culture, and a model train. If you like the layout, visit the National Toy Train Museum (*see above*).

HEY, KIDS! Train terms seem so complicated, but they aren't really. A locomotive is the same as an engine. A coach is just a passenger car with seats; specialized passenger cars can be lounge cars, dining cars, or sleepers, or serve a combination of functions. Freight cars carry goods rather than people. They can be hoppers, which have sloped floors for discharging the loose, dry materials they carry (like grain or coal); tankers, which transport fluids; and boxcars, rectangular cars that usually carry self-contained or packaged goods. So what's rolling stock? It's everything.

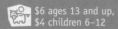

Back on track level, there are a Western Union ticket office, railroad worker mannequins, baggage carts, and other displays, but it's hard to take your eyes off the trains. Kids and kids at heart will want to scamper up and down the platforms looking for those cars that you can actually board. Climb up on freight locomotive 2846 to see all the levers and valves, the steam pressure gauge, and where the fire was stoked. You can pull the chain, but alas, the whistle won't sound. Peer into a mail car to see the sorting bins and mailbags or into the Lotos Club, a combination sleeping/dining/lounge car with an elegantly set dining table, berths, and card table. (A warning from the Pullman Company tells you to beware of con men and card sharks.) Walk through a P-70 passenger coach, with red velvet seats, and a red caboose, the home and office of a freight-train crew. You can even climb up into the cupola and make believe you're keeping an eye out for shifting loads. There's something about a train that's magic.

EATS FOR KIDS   Lunch aboard the Strasburg Rail Road's **Lee Brenner Dining Car** (Rte. 741, tel. 717/687–6486), a converted early 1900s wooden coach. On the 45-minute trip, grown-ups eat soup, sandwiches, or salad, while kids choose between PB&J and hot dog platters. **Isaac's** (Shops at Traintown, Rte. 741 E, tel. 717/687–7699) resembles a train car with flamingos. A flock of sandwiches—named for birds—includes some on soft pretzels. **Strasburg Creamery** (1 W. Main St., tel. 717/687–0766) serves sandwiches and ice cream. Also see the National Toy Train Museum.

RIDLEY CREEK STATE PARK

Only 16 miles from Center City lies a gem called Ridley Creek State Park, bisected by a creek of the same name. Gently rolling terrain is mainly forested, but open space is here, too, as are lovely 18th- to 20th-century stone buildings and fences. The most impressive is a stone mansion with walled-in gardens, which serves as the park office building (lucky rangers!). However, the park is not just another pretty place. Within its over 2,600 acres are a host of recreational opportunities and a functioning, re-created 18th-century farm.

Trail enthusiasts will find 12 miles of hiking trails and 5 miles of paved multiuse (bicycling and jogging) trails, any of which can be used by cross-country skiers. Horseback riders can clip-clop on designated equestrian trails, and Hidden Valley Farm, a stable operated as a concession, offers guided trail rides, hay rides, and pony rides on weekend afternoons. The creek itself, stocked with trout, has an area for fly-fishing, and a hill near the park office has sledding written all over it.

EATS FOR KIDS The park has plenty of picnic groves for lunch al fresco. As for restaurants, the **Country Deli** (1176 N. Middletown Rd., Gradyville, tel. 610/558–3354), on Route 352, usually only serves breakfast and lunch (sandwiches, grill food), but Wednesday and Friday are pasta nights. You can eat outside in nice weather. At **Al E. Gators** (4803 West Chester Pike, Newtown Square, tel. 610/356–7666), out on Route 3, children can color at the table, eat kids' menu fare, and meet the alligator mascot. **Dairy Queen** (5000 West Chester Pike, Edgemont, tel. 610/356–9566) is another nearby, albeit standard, option.

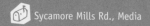 Sycamore Mills Rd., Media

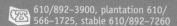 610/892-3900, plantation 610/566-1725, stable 610/892-7260

 Park free; plantation $4 ages 13 and up, $2 children 4-12

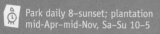 Park daily 8-sunset; plantation mid-Apr-mid-Nov, Sa-Su 10-5

 All ages

What makes Ridley Creek truly unusual is Colonial Pennsylvania Plantation, a 112-acre living-history farm on park property. "Prepare to enter the 18th century," reads a sign at the entrance—more accurately a Quaker farm circa 1760–90. It's a modest farm by today's standards, though the owners would have been considered well-to-do at the time, as evidenced by a center hall and red (the most expensive color) beams in the farmhouse. Restoration of plantation buildings and the running of the farm today are accomplished using 18th-century tools and technology.

Costumed interpreters in the farmhouse try to stay in character, though they do explain the workings of the plantation in a language you can understand. They might scold young girls for scandalously showing their bare elbows or being so vain as to have their hair uncovered. They might even put willing children to work cleaning the table or paddling butter. If you're not so inclined, don't worry; you can just watch. Or wander, unhurried, around these bucolic grounds.

GETTING THERE The park has three entrances: from Route 3 (West Chester Pike), west of Newtown Square, and from Gradyville Road, either east from Route 352 or west from Route 252.

HEY, KIDS! A child's life was very different 200 years ago. Only the littlest children could eat at the table. Older kids would grab food while standing and then go run around. Schooling was done at home, at a desk in the West Parlor, but much of the day was spent working, as no competent child would just sit around. Even 4-year-olds would card wool and spin it into yarn with a drop spindle. And oh yes, children usually had one set of clothes, the bottom layer of which (chemise for girls, nightshirt for boys) they also slept in.

SCHUYLKILL CENTER FOR ENVIRONMENTAL EDUCATION

T ake a peaceful walk through the woods at this 500-acre nature preserve, the largest privately owned open space in Philadelphia. You'll probably forget you're within the city limits—at least until you spy radio antennas and the Center City skyline (on a clear day) above the trees or hear trains, planes, and automobiles in the distance. No matter. Plenty of natural sights and sounds will recapture your attention, including lush greenery, babbling brooks, plentiful wildlife, and ever-present birdsong.

About 8 miles of trails loop through the preserve, offering something for every age. The paved, ¼-mile Widener Trail is both wheelchair- and stroller-friendly. Trail markers are keyed to a handout about succession in the forest. Toddlers can handle the equally short Upper Fields Trail, leading to the seasonal, screened-in Butterfly House. Here delicate creatures fly around you, especially June–August.

Older youths can tackle the 1-mile Ravine Loop (going counterclockwise avoids a steep

EATS FOR KIDS It would be a shame not to "eat out" here in one of the picnic areas. If you didn't pack a lunch, pick up yummy deli sandwiches or hoagies, fresh produce, and snacks at **T & F Farmers Pride** (8101 Ridge Ave., tel. 215/487–0889).

HEY, KIDS! Use all five of your senses. Look for animals, like the groundhog that hangs around near the entrance. Listen for birds, from the tweets of songbirds to the rat-a-tats of woodpeckers. Smell the canisters at the scent table in the Discovery Room. (Can you tell strawberry from watermelon?) Touch—but not any poison ivy. Taste the tubes of flavored honey for sale in the gift shop, like that made by the bees in the center's hive. It just goes to show that nature can be experienced in all sorts of ways.

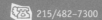 8480 Hagy's Mill Rd.

 $3 ages 13 and up, $2 children 2–12

M–Sa 8:30–5, Su 1–5

215/482-7300

All ages

climb), which takes you well beneath the tree canopy and along a spring-fed stream lined with nature's glitter: mica sand. Keep an eye out for white-tailed deer as they keep an eye out for you, bounding away if you get too close. As you cross a boardwalk over wetlands, look for pairs of frog eyes camouflaged amid water plants. Watch, too, for any evidence animals have left behind—tracks, holes pecked in trees, and even poop—but ignore, and don't contribute to, the unfortunate evidence left by humans: occasional litter and tree carvings. If you're up for more walking, add the Wind Dance Pond and Woodcock trails to your loop, passing the old stone springhouse on your way to the man-made Wind Dance Pond, where parts of Oprah Winfrey's movie *Beloved* were filmed.

Other ways to enjoy the trails here are bimonthly Storybook Strolls (ages 4–12), including stories about the natural world, hikes that explore aspects of each book, and craft activities. In winter, skis come to SCEE—cross-country skis, that is. There's something to do year-round at this undiscovered city wilderness.

KEEP IN MIND "Take nothing but pictures. Leave nothing but footprints." These familiar words of nature wisdom are particularly appropriate here. Bring a camera so your kids can snap photos, adding to their enjoyment and providing them with "legal" mementos of their day in the woods—no picked plants or pocketed rocks, please. Also make sure your kids don't bring home any unwanted souvenirs. Where there are woods and deer, there will be wood and deer ticks. Though fear of ticks should *not* keep you away, be sure to check everyone carefully for hitchhikers after your visit.

SESAME PLACE

Big Bird and his buddies may live on a famous New York City street, but on hot days, you'll find them—along with car- and busloads of others—at a slightly different address. Bucks County's Sesame Place is a water-filled theme park whose theme is Sesame Street. Not surprisingly, it's popular with preschool and elementary schoolkids, who come to cavort in the assortment of tame to moderate water activities and meet their furry and feathered friends in person (or is that "in monster"?).

The Sesame Street motif is carried throughout—from the topiary to the piped-in music. Take your children's picture in front of 123 Sesame Street or posing with a roving, huggable Elmo or Ernie. Water rides, too, have Sesame influences, though it's hard to ponder them while getting dunked. Older kids like Sky Splash (look for Ernie's rubber ducky), a twirling six-person raft ride culminating in a soggy splash-down; Sesame Streak, a turning inner tube ride; and Slippery Slopes and Big Slipper, for those who want nothing to come between them and the cool water. Big Bird's Rambling River—a leisurely tube float with spouts,

KEEP IN MIND Follow basic water-park wisdom. To miss the biggest crowds, avoid hot midsummer weekends. Early September is good, as are rain-dotted days; crowds tend to leave after a shower. Bring warmer clothes if it's cooler or if you tend to get chilled. Go early or stay late (lines get short near closing), and visit popular rides while everyone else is watching the parade. Alas, the mostly student staff is not always adept at keeping lines moving. For a shorter wait for the Rambling River, head for the entrance on Sesame Island, which is through, not in front of, the Good Ship Sesame. Water shoes or Tevas are recommended.

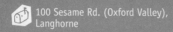

100 Sesame Rd. (Oxford Valley),
Langhorne

215/752-7070

$34.95 ages 2 and up, $18.95
twilight (after 2 when park
open to 5 or 6, after 4 when
open to 7 or 8)

Late May–early Sept, daily; early
Sept–Oct, weekends; hrs vary

2–13

sprays, and squeals—appeals to many ages, while other areas such as Twiddlebug Land, with a shallow wave pool, and Little Bird's Birdbath and not-so-rapid Rapids, are for the youngest visitors. Swim diapers (required) are available at gift shops.

Nonwet activities include Vapor Trail, a small, moderate-thrill roller coaster; the daily parade; and shows ranging from the impressive Pet Pals to a Sesame Street revue. The park's driest corner has a climbing net, air-mattress bounce, and small playground; use it as a break rather than a first stop, or you'll squander too much of your $35 day.

Except for the occasional startled, teary-eyed toddler and a few staff members who seem to have been trained by Oscar the Grouch, Sesame Place is basically a warm, fuzzy (if tiring) experience. At day's end, your kids will probably clamor for one more ride, while you'll be ready for a nap.

GETTING THERE

Take I–95 north past the water tower with Big Bird and his buddies to U.S. 1 North. Exit at Oxford Valley, turning right on Oxford Valley Road. Turn right at the third traffic light into the Oxford Valley Mall, home to acres of retail stores and parking lots.

EATS FOR KIDS

To save money, bring lunch, store it in a locker (a necessity, though poorly designed), and eat in a picnic area. The air-conditioned **Food Factory** serves chicken-strip kids' meals as well as chicken Caesar. Outside the park, chain restaurants suitable for the aprés-splash crowd include **T.G.I. Friday's** (tel. 215/750–8002) and **Red Robin** (tel. 215/752–1000), on the mall service road, and **Pizzeria Uno** (tel. 215/741–6100), **Romano's Macaroni Grill** (tel. 215/949–9990), **Chili's** (tel. 215/943–5555), and **Old Country Buffet** (tel. 215/547–6640), along Oxford Valley Road.

SIX FLAGS GREAT ADVENTURE

Like other Six Flags parks, Great Adventure has carved out a niche as a thrill-seekers' paradise. Your mind might be boggled by the number of rides here (69 and counting), but it'll be numbed, spun, and jiggled by the 10 or so mega-monsters. Naturally, there are plenty of moderate and downright tame rides, too, plus shows, games, and a splash of Looney Tunes characters. But many rides are familiar ones—teacups, bumper cars, swing rides, a Ferris wheel, and a carousel—rather than unusual signature experiences, and the park looks a little worn around the edges. It's like a traveling carnival on steroids.

Though the park's newest mega coaster is dubbed Nitro, most of the higher, steeper, faster, scarier rides tend to be named for deadly creatures and superheroes, like Viper, Medusa, and Batman and Robin: The Chiller. (Can Black Widow Spiderman be far behind?) The park guide adds to your knowledge with such descriptions as "floorless, top-rail looping steel roller coaster" (Medusa) and "steel, heartline inverting roller coaster" (Viper). To really get the picture, though, you have to see them, hear them (riders' screams are plenty

HEY, KIDS!

Coasters not scary enough for you? Come during Fright Fest (late September–October), Six Flags's monthlong Halloween party. The park is decorated for Halloween, shows have a Halloween theme, and there's even a haunted hayride.

KEEP IN MIND Great Adventure is one of three adjacent Six Flags parks (combination tickets available). The newest, Hurricane Harbor is a 45-acre tropical-theme water park with the requisite slides, wave pool, river ride, and family lagoon. Six Flags Wild Safari (*see below*) is a drive-through animal encounter that's such a good time—and only an extra $1 or $2 on top of theme-park admission—that it'd be a shame to miss it. Better watch the clock, though. Cars aren't allowed in after 4, but if you get a hand stamp and save your parking receipt, you can go back to Great Adventure afterward.

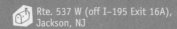 Rte. 537 W (off I–195 Exit 16A), Jackson, NJ

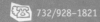 732/928-1821

 $45.99 49" and up, $22.99 48" and under

 Early Apr–early May and early–late Sept, Sa–Su; mid-May–Labor Day, daily; late Sep–Oct, F–Su; hrs vary

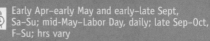 2 and up

audible above the coasters' loud rumbling), and ultimately, ride them.

Smaller thrills warm families up for the biggies. Two park areas, Looney Tunes Seaport and Bugs Bunny Land, are geared for little ones. In the moderate department, Frontier Adventures, a Wild West–theme area, has the Runaway Mine Train and the Saw Mill Log Flume. Shows, including a fun dive show and lakefront stunt spectacular, are nice places to take a break. One of the cleverest and most unusual experiences is Houdini's Great Escape, a simulator ride illusion that feels like—nah, giving it away would spoil the fun.

So is Great Adventure worth it? If you have only little kids, maybe and maybe not. Other local parks are geared more for the swingset set, though the half-price admission for those under 4' goes a long way toward making a day here more affordable. If you have a budding thrill seeker—and a good chiropractor—go for it.

EATS FOR KIDS   There are as many places to find lunch here as there are to lose it. Most food costs about twice what you'd pay in the outside world, however, and leans heavily on the sweet and greasy, and tall drinks come in colors not known in nature. Themed eateries are everywhere. Smelling like the shore experience for which it's named, Boardwalk contains **Mustard's Last Stand** and the **Boardwalk Sugar Shack.** Frontier Adventures has **Best of the West** and **Casa de Taco,** and Main Street serves up the **Great American Hamburger.** Also see Six Flags Wild Safari.

SIX FLAGS WILD SAFARI

Remember how fun it was to drive through a car wash when you were a kid? And that was only soapy water. Wild Safari is, in essence, a drive-through zoo, but even that doesn't do it justice. In most zoos, you are separated from the animals by some distance and, though there may be no visual barrier, you are definitely on the outside looking in. Here, however, the tables are turned. You are on the inside gazing out at creatures that are both curious-looking and just plain curious. They think nothing of going eyeball to eyeball with you to get a better look.

Along the 4½-mile circuit, you can drive as slow or fast as you like, provided it's under 10 mph. Three lanes enable anxious drivers to pass those who want to stop and be stared at. The average drive time is about an hour, but frankly it's a shame to go through that quickly.

Things start slowly with the American section, but don't worry: The animals get more exotic soon. In the next few sections, you might see a peacock leading a parade of cars like a

HEY, KIDS! Why did the water buffalo cross the road? To get to the other side, of course—where there's a delicious water hole to stand in. What's black and white and red all over? Not the zebras here; they're more brown and white. And what's that strange animal that looks like it's part donkey, part deer, and part dog, with a bull's-eye on its rear? Beats me, but it's sure awesome. Have fun looking at all the weird and wonderful animals. Observe their behavior, assuming they're behaving at all. (They might be sleeping.) If they're misbehaving, don't watch. You'll only encourage them.

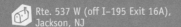

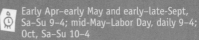
drum major, a camel caravan ambling past, elephants luxuriating in a communal bath, a giraffe stopping traffic with a little rubbernecking, or an ostrich playing peekaboo and occasionally pecking at your window (big eyes, small brain). It should be noted that the elephants, along with the lions and tigers, are in their own enclosures and can't approach your vehicle (whew!).

Continue through bears and birds, Australia and South America, to the grand finale: Monkey Jungle. You haven't lived until you've had an Anubis baboon climb onto your rearview mirror and scratch himself. These bold creatures will swarm hood and roof, doing anything and everything you can imagine—and some things you can't—in a hilarious impersonation of a pack of furry two-year-olds. It's way more fun than a puny barrelful. And it's a good thing this is the last stop, because there's no topping it.

EATS FOR KIDS
You'll find a small drive-up snack stand inside the safari and a picnic area outside. Otherwise, options are mainly fast food on Route 537 between Six Flags and I-195. On the other side of I-195, the **Six Flags Factory Outlets** has a food court.

KEEP IN MIND Believe the warnings about Monkey Jungle! The little monsters can remove car parts faster than an Indy pit crew. Put down antennas, and watch to see if the rascals leave your car with more than they came with: Rubber trim pieces are favorites. Don't feed them (or any safari animals), and don't get out until you clear the exit. Then thoroughly examine your car. If something's missing, tell the gate attendant, who can maybe have it retrieved. If you're really worried about your car, take the bus or the baboon bypass, but they're much less fun—at least until you get the repair bill.

TOWN CRIER SUMMER THEATRE

Many attractions claim to bring history to life, but this assemblage of costumed actors, singers, and reenactors does so better than most. You'll find them roaming the historic district, sporting tricorner hats and petticoats (surely they must be hot!), and staying in character. Chat with Ben Franklin, Betsy Ross, or a less-famous Colonial citizen and watch as the drama of 1774–87 unfolds.

Town Criers consist of two main groups, "towns players" and "townspeople." Ask any of them for a schedule of events—but not in mid-play. Towns players act out playlets, most of which are part of the "American Story," a chronological journey from "Troubling Taxes" to a pageant of flags called "We the People." Feel free to shout "Boo! Hiss!" or "Huzzah!" (hooray), since audience participation is encouraged—especially during the Call to Arms. A fife and drum parade leads children Pied Piper–style to enlist in Gen. Washington's army. Washington himself inspects troops right down to their teeth (to be sure they can bite the end off their powder cartridges) and then drills them with wooden muskets. George

EATS FOR KIDS Depending on where you are in Old City, there's undoubtedly a coffee shop, café, or pizzeria within a block or two. Look for suggestions under listings for actual Old City sights.

KEEP IN MIND Not all the playlets are part of the "American Story" timeline, which takes place in Independence National Historical Park (*see above*). Some chronicle everyday life or tell stories of ethnic groups not covered in standard birth-of-a-nation history. Look for these skits at other nearby sights, including the Atwater Kent Museum (15 S. 7th St.), Philadelphia's history museum; the African American Museum in Philadelphia (701 Arch St.); the National Museum of American Jewish History (55 N. 5th St.); Elfreth's Alley; and Christ Church (2nd St. between Market and Arch Sts.). Many family events are held at the Betsy Ross House (*see above*).

12 locations around Old City

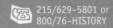 215/629–5801 or
800/76-HISTORY

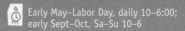 Early May–Labor Day, daily 10–6:00;
early Sept–Oct, Sa–Su 10–6

 All ages

Free

is pretty funny for a general, but don't cross him. He'll threaten to cut off your hand if you talk on your cell phone during training or to put your child in the stocks (locked to a gate) if discipline or commitment is lacking. If kids pass this basic basic training, they get a certificate.

Interspersed among the playlets are performances by the Libertytones, a Colonial singing group in four-part harmony, who might just teach you some Colonial song and dance.

Townspeople, by contrast, are Colonial characters who frequent Old City. Ben and Betsy are among them, but they're mostly regular 18th-century folks with everyday stories to tell—in the language of the time, naturally. Mention a word they don't recognize, such as "kids," and they're apt to respond, "Kids? Are there young goats about?"

So while you're visiting sights, make time for the Town Criers. They'll give you an interesting perspective on Colonial life and make you smile, too. Huzzah!

HEY, KIDS! Before stepping back to the 18th century, spend some time on that 21st-century phenomenon: the Internet. Check out the Town Crier bios on the historic.philly.com web site, and pick some you might want to meet. Remember that each townsperson has a very real identity, so you can keep an eye peeled for your favorite, whether it's a doctor or barmaid, aristocrat or gravedigger, teacher or apothecary, midwife or scoundrel.

TRENTON THUNDER

With several big-league franchises in Philadelphia, why travel to Trenton to watch minor-league baseball? Simply put, though the caliber of play is lower (the Thunder is a double-A Boston Red Sox affiliate), the caliber of affordable, family entertainment is higher.

The Delaware River forms the backdrop for comfortable, intimate Waterfront Park. Parking is easy and only $1, and the park's small capacity—just over 6,400—means you won't have to watch the video screen to know what's happening on the field. But it's off the field that the Thunder makes a special effort. Boomer, the team's bright blue "Thunderbird" mascot (check out those cool thunderbolt shades) galumphs about, shooting T-shirts into the stands with a slingshot, tossing out Frisbees, or catching fans with his fishing net. Kids gravitate to him. You'll chuckle as you watch him race one lucky tot around the bases between innings. Guess who wins?

To try to sign your child up for that or other between-innings promotions—including a

EATS FOR KIDS Going to a ballgame and not eating a hot dog—why, the idea is positively un-American! **Concessions** carry the requisite "Thunder dog," alongside pizza, cheese steaks, burgers, and Italian sausage, at prices about what you'd expect, plus a kids' box. For a less greasy, full-service alternative, walk upriver to the neat old factory building housing **Kat Man Du** (50 Riverview Executive Park, tel. 609/393–7300). A quasi-Caribbean theme extends to but doesn't limit the seasonal menu—from a Reggae Reuben to Primavera Pizza. Huge kids' pizzas and other standbys are safe children's choices. For fun, eat on the deck overlooking the river.

Mercer County Waterfront Park,
1 Thunder Rd. (on Rte. 29), Trenton, NJ

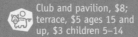 Club and pavilion, $8;
terrace, $5 ages 15 and
up, $3 children 5–14

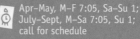 Apr–May, M–F 7:05, Sa–Su 1;
July–Sept, M–Sa 7:05, Su 1;
call for schedule

609/394–TEAM

 3 and up

dizzy bat race, an Operation-type game, and a cheerleading contest—check with Guest Services an hour before game time. In fact, arriving early lets you do several fun things. Enjoy the free moon bounce, balloon-animal makers (warning: hot balloons pop), and brass band in front of the stadium. On Sundays, the first 55 kids (sign up at Guest Services) can join the post-game Sunday Funday Run; after running the bases, participants get a logo baseball and an "Official Contract." Register for Boomer's Buddies Kid's Club, and your kids can attend an on-field clinic taught by Thunder players (five pregame mornings in July and August).

There's plenty to do during the game, too. Aspiring pitchers can test their speed and accuracy at one booth. An arcade has virtual-reality baseball among its video games. And of course, you *can* watch the ballgame, but it's okay to get distracted. Thunder management doesn't care to remember the score as long as you remember to have a great time.

KEEP IN MIND

Other area minor-league or similar teams include the Reading Phillies and new Camden River Sharks (baseball) and the Philadelphia Kixx (soccer), Wings (lacrosse), and Phantoms (ice hockey), which play in the First Union Spectrum or Center. Indoor sports are loud, however, and Phantoms games can get rough.

HEY, KIDS! Want an autograph of a Thunder player? There are a number of ways to get one. Boomer or a player signs autographs in front of the stadium about 45 minutes before each game as well as at the Kid's Club clinics. Hang out by the dugout before the game or at the entrance to the players' hallway 30 to 45 minutes after the game, and you should be able to snag a willing ballplayer. Who knows? Today's players might become tomorrow's stars. It wasn't long ago that batting champ Nomar Garciaparra played for the Thunder.

U OF PENN MUSEUM OF ARCHAEOLOGY AND ANTHROPOLOGY

Give kids a pail and shovel, and they'll dig and dig, unearthing treasures belonging to yesterday's civilizations—or at least yesterday's beachgoers. Now imagine well over a century's worth of Penn archaeologists and anthropologists digging and collecting around the world and amassing a wealth of artifacts. These treasures, only a portion of which are on display due to space constraints, fill this venerable three-story university museum.

Kids gravitate to the Egyptian galleries, located on the first and third floors. In the Lower Egyptian Gallery, you can see the 12-ton granite sphinx of Ramses II and items from the palace of Pharaoh Merenptah (circa 1200 BC). But it's the Upper Egyptian Gallery and its mummies that elicit cries of "Wo!" from amazed youngsters. Egyptians believed their afterlife would be as cool (or, more accurately, as hot) as their life, if only they brought the right stuff with them. The gallery displays items that were entombed with Egyptians, including ushabtis (servant statues waiting to work in the afterlife); a mummified cat; decorated coffins and sarcophagi; and some real mummies. You can

EATS FOR KIDS The **Museum Cafe** is really just a small cafeteria line and a nice glass-walled seating area overlooking inner gardens. Choices include a hot entrée, soup, and sandwiches, including half turkey, tuna, and egg salad sandwiches (about $2). You're also welcome to bring your own food.

HEY, KIDS! Mummification was a long (70-day), expensive process. (Warning: Gross stuff coming up!) Most of the main organs—liver, stomach, intestines, and lungs—were removed and put in special jars, called canopic jars. The heart, however, remained in the body. The brain was removed, too, but not in one piece. A hot hook was passed through the nose, creating a "brain milkshake" that was drained out and discarded. The body was then soaked in a preserving salt called natron, dried, rubbed with oils, and stuffed and wrapped in linen. Don't try this at home. Mummy wouldn't like it.

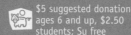
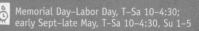

actually see teeth protruding from one wrapped body, black toes from another.

Next to Upper Egypt, the tall, skylit Chinese rotunda has huge impressive pairs of cloisonné lions and stone chimeras, but the centerpiece is a 49-pound crystal ball, the second-largest in the world. You won't see Auntie Em turn into the Wicked Witch, but you will see the room reflected upside down in this giant orb.

Don't ignore the second floor, either. This is where you'll find collections from closer to home, including Living in Balance, about Native Americans of the Southwest, and Raven's Journey, displaying artifacts, including some wonderful masks, from Alaskan peoples. A changing-exhibit area offers a glimpse at pieces from the enormous collection that normally remain in storage. Because of their fresh and contemporary presentations, these temporary exhibits often appeal to kids, and, just as in archaeology, you never know what you'll find.

KEEP IN MIND   The museum has many programs. Two-hour, drop-off programs (8 and up), one Saturday morning a month, entail about an hour in a gallery and an hour for a related project, such as making a mask. Though these programs halt in summer (the building isn't air-conditioned), one-hour Summer Magic sessions, often with performances, are given on selected Wednesday and Thursday mornings instead. Look for public tours and interactive gallery programs, announced by the entrance and, unintelligibly, over the PA system, and for annual cultural event days.

U.S. MINT

Money, or at least the love of it, may be the root of all evil, but watching it being made is just plain fun. Philadelphia's mint is actually one of only two mints in the country—the other is Denver—that coins legal tender. (Other mints make commemorative medals, as does this one.) Presses work around the clock, though the public is only welcome during the day. Taking a self-guided tour will teach your family about the history of coin- and medal-making in the United States and give you a bird's-eye view of the process.

Before heading up the escalator to start your tour, look around the lobby. Two tanks filled with pennies and Delaware quarters are the first tip-off to how much money you'll see being made within this massive edifice. Approximately 40 million coins ($2 million) are made here daily, including the state quarters.

The tour itself takes place in two long halls. In the first, exhibits on the mint and its products actually give a mini-U.S. history lesson. Displays include Commemorative Gold

HEY, KIDS! It helps to know the special terms used at the mint. Blanks? They're the metal discs before they're stamped with designs. Riddling isn't the jokes the mint work-ers tell; it's the process of sorting blanks to remove any that are the wrong size. Upsetting? Not very. Upsetting is the name for raising the rim around the coins' edge. And striking isn't walking out on the job here; it means stamping the designs and inscriptions that make these coins genuine U.S. currency. Just for fun, the next time you're flipping a coin, say, "obverse or reverse": mintspeak for "heads or tails."

 5th and Arch Sts.

 Free

 May–June, M–Sa 9–4:30; July–Aug, M–Sa 9–4:30, Su 11–4:30; Sept–Apr, M–F 9–4:30

 215/408-0114

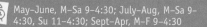 3 and up

Medals for famous Americans from George Washington to Walt Disney and old-fashioned equipment like assay balances. It's interesting background, but the best part of the tour, especially for kids, starts when you do a 180° turn around the wall at the end of the corridor. Suddenly you face a series of windows, which overlooks rows of presses and other machines that are actually manufacturing coins. (By 2002, when the process becomes completely automated, exhibits in the first hallway will be replaced by windows, too.) It's hard to tell exactly what's doing what, but it's still interesting to gaze down on all those coins-to-be as they travel on conveyor belts, into vibrating machines or raging furnaces, and out chutes into gleaming piles. Workers (who are checked when they leave, so they can't pocket any change) attend to the machines, and the action is positively Seussian. Video monitors along this hall describe stages in the minting process and dispense the odd piece of trivia—but alas, no samples.

EATS FOR KIDS
Aside from a small lobby snack stand, the mint sells no food. However, a few blocks down 5th, below Market, the **Bourse food court** (5th St. between Ludlow and Ramstead Sts.) contains a Bain's Deli, Sbarro (pizza), Mandarin Express, Salad Works, and Grand Olde Cheesesteak, among others.

KEEP IN MIND To learn more about money, pull out some change and ask your kids about it. What words are on all coins? Which coin doesn't say how much it's worth in cents or dollars? Which coins were made here? Philadelphia-made coins have a "P" (heads side, lower right) or no letter; those from Denver have a "D." But perhaps the best economics lesson happens at tour's end, when you enter a gift shop with every flavor of mint memorabilia imaginable. Most kids like dropping a few coins on a few coin-related items, and they'll soon learn how far today's dollar goes.

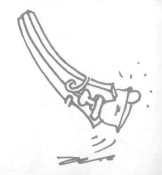

U.S.S. NEW JERSEY NAVAL MUSEUM & VETERAN'S MEMORIAL

5

Dropping anchor along the shores of the state for which she was named and across from the shipyard where she was built, the U.S.S. *New Jersey* has a brand-new mission. But this tour of duty is educational rather than military. The mighty Iowa-class battleship, also known as BB-62, is opening her watertight doors to visitors. In so doing, she'll teach various generations about her storied past, about life aboard ship, and about how something so big can feel so small.

Launched during World War II and recommissioned twice before being finally decommissioned in 1991, the *New Jersey* reopens in September 2001. Though long-term plans (2002–03) call for a full land-side interpretive museum covering topics from naval architecture to battleship history and including interactive exhibits and a large-format theater, the original shore facility will consist of a welcome center and gift shop.

After stopping at the welcome center, walk out the pier to the ship herself. Initially,

EATS FOR KIDS Initially, the welcome center will sell snack food, but as the museum develops, a food court serving inexpensive fare will open. From here you'll be able to gaze at the ship and the active South Jersey Port. *Also see* New Jersey State Aquarium & Children's Garden.

KEEP IN MIND The battleship is just one of many new and planned developments along the Camden Waterfront, making it possible to spend a very full day just across the river from Philadelphia. What began with the aquarium and later the E-Centre and children's garden is continuing full speed ahead. Joining the RiverLink Ferry as a scenic way to cross the river, an aerial tram is slated for 2003. Not far from the live Jaws, the Camden River Sharks play minor-league baseball, and an entertainment complex with 3-D IMAX theater and an aquarium expansion are on the drawing board. For information, check out www.camdenwaterfront.com.

just the main deck and first five levels will be accessible, but don't worry: There's plenty to see in these rabbit-warren-like spaces. Much is officers' country, including spacious captain's and admiral's staterooms (bedrooms) that contrast with lesser mortals' stacked bunks, wardrooms (dining rooms), and heads (bathrooms). You can also tour the communications center, conning station, and gun turret 1, home to the enormous 16" guns that gave the *New Jersey* the nickname "Firepower for Freedom." Since the ship was restored to her 1983 appearance, Tomahawk missile canisters are also on board.

Due to the small corridors, you're asked to follow the arrow-marked tour. Narrow, steep stairs and watertight bulkheads require agility; keeping to the deck and other easily accessible areas is recommended for those unsteady on their feet. Uniformed volunteers, including some former battleship sailors, answer questions and sometimes perform reenactments, as even today, the *New Jersey* inspires intense reverence and loyalty. More than a few tears have been shed in welcoming her back.

HEY, KIDS! This is one big lady—all 887 feet of her. Her anchor weighs two tons, and each link of its chain is 90 pounds. Those 16-inch guns could shoot a 2,700-pound shell 25 miles, and it took 65 sailors to man each turret. No problem. In the ship's heyday, there were nearly 3,000 men—no women—aboard (55,000 over her career). Imagine 3,000 guys below deck with no air-conditioning and only 2 gallons of freshwater daily. Sound like a lot? Imagine 2 gallons for drinking, washing clothes, and showering. Still, despite the lack of creature comforts, sailors gladly served on the battleship for years.

VALLEY FORGE NATIONAL HISTORICAL PARK

Ask people to name famous places from the American Revolution, and Valley Forge invariably makes the list. Ask why it's famous, and the mumbling begins, usually including something about winter. What's ironic for a historic war site is that no battle was fought at Valley Forge. Site of a six-month encampment for Washington's weary troops—through the harsh winter and spring of 1777–78—it was the scene of suffering, sacrifice, and, ultimately, the rebirth of the Continental Army.

As at any historical park, the place to start is the visitor center, where you can watch an 18-minute film and buy tickets for Washington's Headquarters. From here on, however, the best part of the history lesson isn't the names and dates; it's seeing what army life was really like. In fact, the only rangers you'll see dressed like Smokey the Bear are at the visitor center; elsewhere, they wear clothes of the time.

If you choose to drive the rolling hills of Valley Forge, follow signs for the 10-mile

EATS FOR KIDS Picnicking is allowed in three picnic areas. The only food sold within the park (though actually on private property) is the hot dogs, pizza, sandwiches, home-made soups, baked goods, and ice cream available at the **Chapel Cabin Shop** (behind Washington Memorial Chapel, tel. 610/783–0576). The King of Prussia Mall (U.S. 202 at Mall Blvd.), just up Gulph Road, has a good number of the restaurant chains, including **Bennigan's** (tel. 610/337–0633), **Dick Clark's American Bandstand Grill** (tel. 610/337–9096), **Houlihan's** (tel. 610/337–9522), and **Ruby's** (tel. 610/337–7829). Every other franchise can probably be found on the roads around the mall.

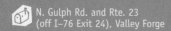 N. Gulph Rd. and Rte. 23
(off I–76 Exit 24), Valley Forge

 610/783-1077

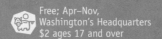 Free; Apr–Nov,
Washington's Headquarters
$2 ages 17 and over

 Park daily sunrise–sunset; visitor center
and Washington's Headquarters daily
9–5; other sights seasonal hrs

 5 and up

Encampment Tour. Cyclists should take the multipurpose trail, which hits the high points in about half the mileage. Another option is a ranger-led walk to the Muhlenberg Brigade, which usually ends with a musket firing.

At the reconstructed mud-chinked huts of the Muhlenberg Brigade, costumed rangers show how soldiers lived: cooking over fire or in the earth-covered oven and sleeping in three-high bunks. Washington's Headquarters seems comparatively spacious—certainly more plush—but in its five rooms, 20-plus people lived and worked. Kids usually eye the period furniture for a minute, but tell them the handrail they're touching is the same one George and Martha touched 2¼ centuries ago, and their eyes get a lot bigger. Other officers' quarters and an artillery park tell more of the story. By mid-June 1778, fortified and retrained by Gen. von Steuben, the army departed, ready to pursue the British. Come on a nice day, and you'll recharge, too.

KEEP IN MIND
Though the visitor center and Washington's Headquarters have consistent hours year-round, the hours of other sights change seasonally. The Muhlenberg Brigade is staffed daily in summer, weekends off-season. Varnum's Quarters is open May–September, while De-wees' House stays open into the winter. Artillery Park has rangers on Sundays June–August.

HEY, KIDS! You can probably imagine grown men encamped here, but can you imagine women and children living here, too? Sometimes it was safer for families to come along with soldiers, especially if their home had been destroyed or their town was occupied by the British. In return for helping with nursing, laundry, and mending, wives were given half rations, and children shared their parents' food. It's not that surprising that because of the cold, lack of food and clothing, and diseases (which spread quickly in such close quarters), 2,000 people died here without a bullet being fired in anger.

WASHINGTON CROSSING HISTORIC PARK

I f most pictures are worth a thousand words, then the well-known painting of George Washington crossing the Delaware is worth considerably more. Because of that painting, most of us know that Washington's Christmas 1776 river crossing was a significant event in the American Revolution—if not why it was significant. To discover the latter, you need only pay a visit to this state park, in a hamlet of the same name.

The history of the crossing is told in a 20-minute film at the visitor center, in the park's southern, McConkey's Ferry section. Historic buildings here, including McConkey's Ferry Inn (where Washington is believed to have eaten Christmas dinner), can be seen on a 45-minute tour, recommended for older children. You'll probably see as many people unloading bikes from their cars as entering the visitor center, however, as cycling the gravel towpath along the nearby canal is as popular a pastime as learning about American history.

HEY, KIDS!
Try to persuade your parents to come on Christmas Day, when costumed re-enactors re-create Washington's river crossing in Durham boat replicas. Busy on Christmas? Come the second Sunday in December, when a festival comes with crafts, decorated houses, and the crossing's dress rehearsal.

EATS FOR KIDS
At the southern section, the **Washington Crossing Inn** (Rtes. 32 and 532, tel. 215/493–3634) is a nice restaurant; dress is casual, but with small children, coming for lunch and sitting on the patio are recommended. For a completely casual experience, pick **Dominick's Pizza** (Washington Crossing Rd., tel. 215/493–1376) or the **Washington Crossing Deli** (1097 Gen. Greene Rd., tel. 215/493–9689), for takeout. Near the tower, **Bourbon Street** (1600 River Rd., New Hope, tel. 215/862–9477) serves bistro cuisine. The town of New Hope is a short, pretty drive up Route 32 (River Road). See New Hope & Ivyland Railroad.

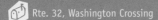

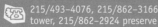
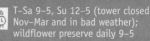
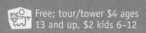
The park's northern Thompson's Mill section is home to another historic 18th-century home used by Continental forces: the Thompson-Neely House. Sheep graze in the pasture outside, and a restored 19th-century gristmill can be seen nearby. Up the hill is 110-foot-high Bowman's Hill Tower, a 1930 fieldstone structure. You can take an elevator almost to the top; 23 narrow steps remain, symbolic of the 23 soldiers who died of illness around the time of the crossing. From the top of the tower, you can see the flagpole near their riverside graves (which you can also visit). If you can ignore the tract mansions, the view from the top is lovely, especially in fall. On a clear day, you can see all the way to the Pennsylvania Turnpike bridge in the south and to Haycock Mountain, in the north.

Bowman's Hill is also the site of a charming wildflower preserve (run independetly of the park) that is attempting to nurture the flowers that were here before the Colonists arrived. Together this cluster of sights makes for a good day of historical re-creation and modern recreation.

KEEP IN MIND To learn more about post-crossing events, check out other local sights. There's another Washington Crossing park (Rte. 546, tel. 609/737–0623) on the Jersey side, with its own visitor center, nature center, trails, and a summer open-air theater. Follow George's route to Trenton's Old Barracks Museum (Barrack St., tel. 609/396–1776), where he surprised the hung-over Hessians the morning after Christmas for a needed victory. If you still aren't Washingtoned out, visit Brandywine Battlefield State Park (U.S. 1, Chadds Ford, tel. 610/459–3342) and Valley Forge (see above).

WHEATON VILLAGE

Enter this southern New Jersey "village" and look down. Shards of glass embedded in the pavement are the first tip-off of the focus here: glass. Thanks to plentiful pine woods (used to stoke the furnaces) and silica-rich sand (the main ingredient of glass), South Jersey was an important glassmaking region, starting in the mid-18th century. That history, and the art of glassmaking, is preserved and interpreted at this center for American crafts.

Glassmaking demonstrations at the T. C. Wheaton Glass Factory let you watch (and, on hot days, sweat) as artists gather molten glass onto hollow pipes for blowing or pontil (solid) rods for molding or finishing. They work fast, rotating the glass to keep it on center while they magically transform glowing red blobs into pitchers and paperweights. In between, they dance back and forth to reheating chambers, called glory holes, to keep the glass hot. FYI, the working temperature of glass is a balmy 2100°F.

Other crafts, too, are represented. Along Crafts and Trades Row, you can watch artisans

EATS FOR KIDS You can bring lunch and eat in the picnic grove or get snacks at vending machines behind the paperweight shop. The **General Store** also sells packaged snack food, but the real reasons to come are the jars of penny candy and the neat old-time atmosphere. Adjacent to the village is the appropriately named **PaperWaiter Restaurant** (111 Village Dr., tel. 856/825–4000), with a full menu of salads, burgers, and all kinds of sandwiches, from wraps and pockets to subs and clubs. A children's menu is available.

1501 Glasstown Rd.
(off Rte. 55 Exit 26), Millville, NJ

856/825-6800 or
800/998-4552

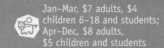
Jan–Mar, $7 adults, $4
children 6–18 and students;
Apr–Dec, $8 adults,
$5 children and students

Jan–Mar, W–Su 10–5 (train and trades
bldg closed); Apr–Dec, daily 10–5;
glassmaking 11, 1:30, and 3:30

5 and up

throwing at potter's wheels, carving wood, and making flame-worked glass (small objects, such as figures, beads, and marbles made from glass rods with a torch). Not far away, a tinsmith demonstrates his craft on weekends.

Kids enjoy riding a ½ scale 1863 train replica through the woods, peeking in a one-room schoolhouse, visiting a stained-glass studio (hours vary), pausing at a playground, and, yes, even touring the Museum of American Glass. While parents are reminded of life before plastic, children can follow the Millie the Mouse Hunt for Cheese, a well-done scavenger hunt that gets kids to look for some pretty unusual and varied articles of glass. Don't worry; everything here is behind either glass or a railing, so no "oopsies" are possible. At the end of the hunt, children are rewarded with a mouse hand stamp and a glimpse of Millie by her mouse hole, and the whole family is rewarded with about a half-day of entertainment and learning.

KEEP IN MIND Were you bitten by the glass-blowing bug? Hot Soup (26 S. Strawberry St., Philadelphia, tel. 215/922–2332), between Market and Chestnut, is the city's only public-access glassblowing studio and gallery. Come watch any day but Thursday (closed August), or visit on First Friday, when there are demonstrations.

HEY, KIDS! Don't just blow through Millie the Mouse. Really look at, and think about, the glass items—including those not on the hunt. In the bottle room, for example, find three bottles with marbles in their necks. Long before screw tops, some bottles were closed with marbles, which floated when the bottle was full. Trouble is, kids would break the bottles to get the marbles. Among the museum's newer glass is the world's largest bottle, blown here in 1992, and the hunt's last item: the beaker. Get the joke? (Hint: A beaker is a deep, wide-mouthed container; so, why the noses?)

THE WISSAHICKON

The pretty Wissahickon Creek plays Cinderella to its bigger, bolder stepsisters: the Delaware and the Schuylkill. Hidden away in a leafy gorge in northwestern Philadelphia, it goes about its business, flowing through some of the city's most picturesque acreage and attracting nature and recreation enthusiasts to its shores.

You can buy a map of the Wissahickon valley from the Valley Green Inn, a charming restaurant about midway down the creek. The map lists sights along the creek, like an Indian statue and covered bridge, but they can easily escape notice if you, like countless others, are whizzing past on your bike. Cyclists, joggers, walkers—and the occasional horseback rider—travel the western bank's wide gravel road, called Forbidden Drive (or, more appropriately, "Forbidden to Drive"). You can even arrange for hayrides or carriage or sleigh rides with Dougherty Carriage Co. (tel. 215/248–4490). In some places the drive descends near water's edge; at others it rises on a cliff. In total, Forbidden Drive is 7 miles long within Fairmount Park, with only one cross-street (Bell's Mill Road) between the city limits and Manayunk.

HEY, KIDS!
Ducks congregate in the creek outside the Valley Green Inn. You can bring food to feed them (please no junk food or anything that will hurt them). If you forget, see if the inn lobby has its customary basket of rolls for people to use.

KEEP IN MIND
Other nature centers provide exhibits, guided walks, and other programs. Depending on where you live, check out Briar Bush Nature Center (1212 Edge Hill Rd., Abington, tel. 215/887–6630), Churchville Nature Center (501 Churchville La., Churchville, tel. 215/357–4005), Peace Valley Nature Center (170 Chapman Rd., Doylestown, tel. 215/345–7860), Pennypack Environmental Center (8600A Verree Rd., tel. 215/685–0470), Riverbend Environmental Education Center (1950 Spring Mill Rd., Gladwyne, tel. 610/527–5234), or the Stony Brook–Millstone Watershed (31 Titus Mill Rd., Pennington, NJ, tel. 609/737–7592).

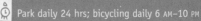

 Along Wissahickon Creek,
Northwestern Ave. to Lincoln Dr.

 Free

Park daily 24 hrs; bicycling daily 6 AM–10 PM

215/685–0000 Fairmount
Park Commission

All ages

On the east bank, a hiker's path wends its way, passing more creek sights and providing entry points for wading canines. Elsewhere in the Wissahickon, the Tree House (Northwestern Ave., tel. 215/685–9285) is the Andorra Natural Area's nature center. You can pick up a map for a self-guided tour or look at the modest exhibits, including a tree cookie (cross-section) of the giant sycamore that once stood here; count the rings back to 1741.

Also just off the creek, Historic RittenhouseTown (206 Lincoln Dr., tel. 215/438–5711), on the small Paper Mill Run, is the site of America's first paper mill, which sounds more industrial than it is. You can watch a film about the original mill, look at exhibits, and visit the homestead/bake house. Come on a day when there are papermaking classes, and you can stay for hours. But leave enough time and energy to bike or walk back to your starting point, lest you turn into a pumpkin.

EATS FOR KIDS   The **Valley Green Inn** (Valley Green Rd. and Wissahickon Creek, tel. 215/247–1730) has a snack bar with hot dogs and other treats; frankly, the inn's restaurant is just too nice a place for sweaty cyclists. On Northwestern Avenue, **Bruno's** (see Morris Arboretum) is a popular destination (or starting point) near the drive's northern end. At the southern end, try **Dalessandro's Steaks** (600 Wendover St., tel. 215/482–5407)—cheese steaks, that is—or pick one of the trendy eateries along Manayunk's Main Street.

THE CLASSICS

"I'M THINKING OF AN ANIMAL..." With older kids you can play 20 Questions: Have your leader think of an animal, vegetable, or mineral (or, alternatively, a person, place, or thing) and let everybody else try to guess what it is. The correct guesser takes over as leader. If no one figures out the secret within 20 questions, the first person goes again. With younger children, limit the guessing to animals and don't put a ceiling on how many questions can be asked. With rivalrous siblings, just take turns being leader. Make the game's theme things you expect to see at your day's destination.

"I SEE SOMETHING YOU DON'T SEE AND IT IS BLUE." Stuck for a way to get your youngsters to settle down in a museum? Sit them down on a bench in the middle of a room and play this vintage favorite. The leader gives just one clue—the color—and everybody guesses away.

FUN WITH THE ALPHABET

"I'M GOING TO THE GROCERY..." The first player begins, "I'm going to the grocery and I'm going to buy... " and finishes the sentence with the name of an object, found in grocery stores, that begins with the letter "A". The second player repeats what the first player has said, and adds the name of another item that starts with "B". The third player repeats everything that has been said so far and adds something that begins with "C" and so on through the alphabet. Anyone who skips or misremembers an item is out (or decide up front that you'll give hints to all who need 'em). You can modify the theme depending on where you're going that day, as "I'm going to X and I'm going to see..."

"I'M GOING TO ASIA ON AN ANT TO ACT UP." Working their way through the alphabet, players concoct silly sentences stating where they're going, how they're traveling, and what they'll do.

FAMILY ARK Noah had his ark—here's your chance to build your own. It's easy: Just start naming animals and work your way through the alphabet, from antelope to zebra.

WHAT I SEE, FROM A TO Z In this game, kids look for objects in alphabetical order—first something whose name begins with "A", next an item whose name begins with "B", and so on. If you're in the car, have children do their spotting through their own window. Whoever gets to Z first wins. Or have each child play to beat his own time. Try this one as you make your way through zoos and museums, too.

PLAY WHILE YOU WAIT

NOT THE GOOFY GAME Have one child name a category. (Some ideas: first names, last names, animals, countries, friends, feelings, foods, hot or cold things, clothing.) Then take turns naming things that fall into that category. You're out if you name something that doesn't belong in the category—or if you can't think of another item to name. When only one person remains, start again. Choose categories depending on where you're going or where you've been—historic topics if you've seen a historic sight, animal topics before or after the zoo, upside-down things if you've been to the circus, and so on. Make the game harder by choosing category items in A-B-C order.

DRUTHERS How do your kids really feel about things? Just ask. "Would you rather eat worms or hamburgers? Hamburgers or candy?" Choose serious and silly topics—and have fun!

BUILD A STORY "Once upon a time there lived..." Finish the sentence and ask the rest of your family, one at a time, to add another sentence or two. Bring a tape recorder along to record the narrative—and you can enjoy your creation again and again.

GOOD TIMES GALORE

WIGGLE & GIGGLE Give your kids a chance to stick out their tongues at you. Start by making a face, then have the next person imitate you and add a gesture of his own—snapping fingers, winking, clapping, sneezing, or the like. The next person mimics the first two and adds a third gesture, and so on.

JUNIOR OPERA During a designated period of time, have your kids sing everything they want to say.

THE QUIET GAME Need a good giggle—or a moment of calm to figure out your route? The driver sets a time limit and everybody must be silent. The last person to make a sound wins.

THE A-LIST

BEST IN TOWN
Grounds for Sculpture
Morris Arboretum
New Jersey State Aquarium & Camden Children's Garden
Philadelphia Zoo
Six Flags Wild Safari

BEST OUTDOORS
Morris Arboretum

BEST CULTURAL ACTIVITY
People's Light & Theatre Company Family Discovery Series

BEST MUSEUM
Franklin Institute

WACKIEST
Philadelphia Insectarium

NEW & NOTEWORTHY
U.S.S. *New Jersey* Naval Museum & Veteran's Memorial

SOMETHING FOR EVERYONE

SCIENCE SCENES

SPORTS STOPS

TINIEST TOTS

TIRE THEM OUT

WATER, WATER EVERYWHERE

WAY UP HIGH

MANY THANKS!

Even small books bear the imprints of many hands. Thanks to all the PR people, educators, and directors at these attractions. Providing information may be your jobs, but you do it with boundless enthusiasm for sharing your treasures. Thanks to my editor, Linda Cabasin, and everyone else at Fodor's who turned manuscript to book. Lisa Oppenheimer, your advice, encouragement, and humor—especially meaningful because you've been there, done that—helped immeasurably. WWLD will be with me for good. My undying gratitude to all the friends, family, and fellow parents who shared their stories and suggestions and to the Newtown Friends School classes of 2004 and 2007, who continually surprised me with their unusual perspectives. Thanks to my merry band of research assistants—Caroline, Lauren, Kate, Fran, Rebekah, Imani, Grace, Kristi, Katherine, Gabrielle, Laura, Ben, Hannah, Sarah, Eva, Ben, Alexis, Melissa, and Junior Troop 805—with extra special thanks to the two best helpers a mom could ask for. Emma and Willa, incredible troopers both, it was amazingly fun to share my work with you. But most of all to my wonderful husband, Andy—chauffeur, cook, moral support, and all-around good egg. There are countless counts for which I'd like to thank you, but I couldn't possibly account for them all.

—Andrea Lehman

the end